The Poet Edgar Allan Poe

The Poet Edgar Allan Poe

Alien Angel

Jerome McGann

Harvard University Press
Cambridge, Massachusetts
London, England
2014

First Printing

Chapter 4 is a composite of two previously published articles:
"Poe. The Politics of a Poetry without Politics," *Literature Compass* 10, 11
(November 2013): 871–884, copyright © 2013 by Jerome McGann; and
" 'The Bells,' Performance, and the Politics of Poetry," *The Edgar Allan Poe
Review* 15, no. 1 (Spring 2014): 47–58, copyright © 2014 by Jerome McGann.

Library of Congress Cataloging-in-Publication Data

McGann, Jerome J., author.
 The Poet Edgar Allan Poe : Alien Angel / Jerome McGann.
     pages cm
 Includes bibliographical references and index.
 ISBN 978-0-674-41666-6
 1. Poe, Edgar Allan, 1809–1849—Poetic works.   2. Poe, Edgar Allan,
1809–1849—Criticism and interpretation.   3. American poetry—
History and criticism.   I. Title.
 PS2642.P63M34 2014
 818'.309—dc23

                                        2014011683

This book is for J. Gerald Kennedy,

the angel of Poe and American Studies

Contents

Abbreviations

CT Poe, Edgar Allan. *Critical Theory: The Major Documents.*
    Edited by Stuart Levine and Susan F. Levine. Urbana
    and Chicago: University of Illinois Press, 2009.

E   Poe, Edgar Allan. *Eureka.* Edited by Stuart Levine and
    Susan F. Levine. Urbana and Chicago: University of
    Illinois Press, 2004.

ER Poe, Edgar Allan. *Essays and Reviews.* Edited by
    G. R. Thompson. New York: Library of America, 1984.

M   Poe, Edgar Allan. *Marginalia.* Edited by John Carl
    Miller. Charlottesville: University Press of Virginia, 1981.

Mabbott Poe, Edgar Allan. *The Collected Works of Edgar Allan
    Poe.* Vol. 1, *Poems.* Edited by Thomas Ollive Mabbott.
    Cambridge MA: Belknap Press, Harvard UP, 1969.

The Poet Edgar Allan Poe

Introduction

❧

*My dear Degas, one does not make poetry with ideas,
but with words.*

Stéphane Mallarmé

In America, Poe's poetry has had a rough ride, as Emerson's sneering quip about "The Jingle Man" testifies.[1] The fact that the poetry has always kept its popular audience has been a persistent academic annoyance, although that problem could be, and has been, effectively controlled with a camp consciousness. The serious scandal of the poetry remains, however, because of the serious admiration it drew from the innovative poetic masters of the next generation: in particular Baudelaire, Whitman, Rossetti, Swinburne, Mallarmé, Remy de Gourmont, and—later still—from Valéry and William Carlos Williams.

Nearly as scandalous as the poetry are the critical and theoretical writings, since they are so closely tied to the poetry. What canonical American poet besides Williams has judged Poe's poetry as important as, say, Whitman's or Dickinson's? (Actually, the answer to that question is T. S. Eliot—a surprising, perhaps a shocking, fact since Eliot delivered some of the harshest comments on Poe's poetry ever written, and since Williams so disapproved Eliot's Modernism.) And while persons as distinguished as Edmund

1

Wilson regard Poe as the first great American critic and poetic theorist, Poe's criticism and theory get discounted as well: besides Wilson, what eminent American literary figure has judged his work as important as Coleridge's or even Wordsworth's?[2] (Actually, the answer to that question is once again T. S. Eliot.)

Imaginative writers regularly struggle against the demands of their office, some openly—Villon, Emily Dickinson, Mandelstam—some obliquely—Virgil, Shakespeare, Jane Austen. Others—Pope is a great instance—grow into their disaffections, turning savage. What a gulf stands between *Windsor Forest* and *The Dunciad*. Poe is perhaps a special case because his work, and in particular the poetry, is at once unremittingly vulgar and theoretically advanced, even pretentious. Fastidious spirits like Emerson, James, and Eliot have had great difficulty managing that fundamental contradiction. Of these Eliot was perhaps the most interesting, being driven over the course of many years to think and rethink the phenomenon of Poe.

That Eliot spent his life wrestling with Poe's poetry is a fact conveniently forgotten in American academic studies. We well remember how greatly he disapproved Poe's verse, forgetting how well he understood that "the influence of his poetry and of his poetic theories [was] immense"—indeed, was a key shaping spirit of the poetical and cultural work that Eliot most admired.[3] In his puzzlement Eliot finally wondered whether Poe all along might have been a secret influence on his own poetry.

At the heart of these problems is the modernity of Poe's severe aesthetic formalism, an approach made famous by what he called "the heresy of *The Didactic*" (*CT* 182). Poetry in his view should not be approached as a repository of ideas or an expression of feelings but as an event of language. For Poe, semantic meanings—denotative or connotative, referential or symbolistic—should be deployed by poets and received by readers as elements in an artistic composition. When Walter Pater subsequently argued that "all art constantly aspires towards the condition of music," he was pledging his allegiance to Poe.[4] So was Samuel Beckett when he declared at the end of *Watt:* "No symbols where none intended." Poe's work lives at the intersection of the bookish Pater and the mischievous Beckett.

Like many after him, Emerson recoiled from what seemed to him Poe's refusal of the serious moral vocation of art. Indeed, Poe's aesthetic stance can appear especially egregious within the fraught political and social world of antebellum America. But the truth is that Poe's work undertakes a deep critical reflection of— and therefore *on*—his period's ethics and politics—as deep as Emily's Dickinson's, with whose work his has much in common, though their radically different life circumstances obscure their similar approaches to poetic expression. Both are poets who, as Dickinson would say, "died for beauty."

These difficulties were shrewdly addressed by two of America's most important poets, neither of whose work looks anything like Poe's. Both Walt Whitman and William Carlos Williams wrote essays on Poe in which he is presented as a regulative force in American culture.[5] For Whitman, Poe is the "center and victim" of what Whitman called the "malady" of America. But committed to offering this "pathological" America a poetic example of social and cultural well-being, Whitman had difficulty understanding the "significance" of a poetry that, while "brilliant and dazzling," had (alas, for Whitman) no "heat." So his essay finishes on a series of puzzled questions about the politics of Poe's "technical and abstract beauty." And they are questions because the principal argument of the essay, rarely acknowledged, is that for Whitman, Poe is "the next best [to Whitman himself] to fully exemplifying" the special power of poets to "diagnose" "this disease called humanity." Whitman "fully admit[s]" this but can't explain for himself "what [it] mean[s]" or how exactly it happens.

Whitman's problem with Poe is Williams's subject. Poe's aesthetic "method" is the "ground" and "beginning" of American imagination, Williams says, exactly because of its theoretical and methodological focus, which "has turned [his work] from mere heat to light" (232), "from sentiment to form" (221). Poe's "method" deploys a "detached . . . abstract [and] cold" poetic expression (231) in order to expose "the grotesque inappropriateness of the life about him" (220). "*Surrounded* by his time" and its crude "utilitarian" materialism," Poe as exemplary writer "*had first to lift his head through* [the] successful banality" (226) of America, had first to become the "center and victim" Whitman recognized. What Whitman obscurely saw Williams will explain. Stripping language back to its "elemental qualities" (221), Poe achieved an imaginative "luminosity that comes of a dissociation from anything else than thought and ideals" (224). The point was to "let the real business of composition *show*" (230), thereby "illustrating his [Poe's] favorite theory that the *theory includes the practice*" (228).

But if Williams grasps Poe's work as a theoretical practice, we can easily mistake his explanation of its real compositional business, that arresting display of "words [and] ideas [that seem] to fall back continuously to a bare surface" (Williams 224). This is a danger for us because, like Whitman, Williams maps the action of the writing to Poe's life and his "battle" against the vulgarity of "his place and time." The writing, "especially . . . the poetry," becomes for him the exponent of "the desperate situation of [Poe's] own mind," the mirror of pathological America. Whitman's "demoniac" poet resurfaces in Williams "in the full horror of his isolation": the poet "driven to be heard by the battering racket about him to a distant screaming" (233).

Be careful with that striking remark. It is an imaginative figure, not a biographical fact. But because it draws upon a recognizable history of Poe and his time, its theoretical significance can be mistaken. Williams is not reheating the cool formalities of Poe's compositional practice; he is sketching the fundamental dynamic of the work. Certainly the writings, not least the poetry, unfold many kinds of demoniac representations, but always in cold, unmoving, and unmoved forms. The writing itself is not expressive, it is *composed*. It takes a zero-degree focus on the reader and readers' responses, where the pathologies of America lie deceptively concealed.

That is why Swinburne called Poe "the complete man of genius."[6] Like Whitman, he sought and found a complete theory of his writing and its social function. It was a very different theory from Whitman's, but as Whitman himself came to recognize, it was at least as thoroughgoing, and—for better or for worse—a good deal more rigorous. Because Poe's relevant poetic corpus is, if we except *Eureka,* so much smaller than Whitman's (or for that matter, Dickinson's), we might judge it less important than theirs. So we would say, I think justly, that among English Romantics, Blake, Wordsworth, Shelley, and Byron are more important than Keats. But Keats's work possesses such striking virtues that he is not displaced from their company. Poe is a similar case—except that his historical position, as Eliot understood, commands a global consequence, as Keats's does not.

The problems here arise and persist, I believe, because Poe's poetic theory and practice depart from the poetical line that descends from what scholars call High Romanticism, which remains dominant in our academy and schools. Indeed, Poe resists that line by radically transforming it. So if we locate Poe in a nineteenth-century context, as we should, conventional touchstones like Wordsworth and Coleridge are most useful—for understanding Poe at any rate—as points of contrast. For comparative purposes we should read Poe's critical work in company with Shelley's, Hallam's, Swinburne's, and Mallarmé's, all of whom think about poetry along *Poetic* lines. Poe stands out, however, even from Shelley, because of the intimate connection between his theoretical writings and his poetic practice. In this respect Swinburne and Mallarmé are alone his peers. All of Poe's significant poetry is a performative demonstration of his theoretical ideas. No American poet ever realized more completely Gertrude Stein's program of "Composition as Explanation."

Poe admired Coleridge's theoretical writings. If we shift our view of Coleridge's work from the normative academic perspective—important as that is in its own right—I believe we can improve our grasp of Coleridge, of Poe, of Romanticism, and finally of the place of poetry in our contemporary world, for which Poe is such an important precursor. That last—poetry's place in the world—is the subject that embraces all the others in this little book. Since I will be taking Poe's poetry as the key to that larger subject, an excursus here into Coleridge or, least of all, Romanticism, would distract from my purpose. Both will make regular appearances in this study. But a brief reflection at this point on Coleridge, "Kubla Khan," and the *Biographia Literaria* may help to throw Poe's work into a new and clearer light.

For both men, plagiarism was pivotal. I do not raise the matter as a moral or a legal issue but as a sign of their extreme sensitivity to and interest in language as such. Poe's accusations against Longfellow are infamous not least because his own work—poetry and prose alike—is a virtual echo chamber of allusions, quotations, and near quotations. More outrageously, he parades himself as an original thinker and polymath when in fact he is a literary privateer. Most astonishing of all, he will call his readers' attention to these matters in ways that cannot fail to recoil on himself. If the Long Longfellow War is the most celebrated example, a marginalium on the quasi-legendary sixteenth-century Scot prodigy James "The Admirable" Crichton (1560?–1582) fairly takes one's breath away:[7]

> Here is a good idea for a Magazine paper:—let somebody "work it up:"—A flippant pretender to universal acquirement—a would-be Crichton—engrosses, for an hour or two perhaps, the attention of a large company—most of whom are profoundly impressed by his knowledge. He is very witty, in especial, at the expense of a modest young gentleman, who ventures to make no reply, and who, finally, leaves the room as if overwhelmed with confusion;—the Crichton greeting his exit with a laugh. Presently he returns, followed by a footman carrying an armful of books. These are deposited on the table. The young gentleman, now, referring to some pencilled notes which he had been secretly taking during the Crichton's display of erudition, pins the latter to his statements, each by each, and refutes them all in turn, by reference to the very authorities cited by the egotist himself—whose ignorance at all points is thus made apparent. (*Marginalia* April 1849, M 174)

As we know, Poe is both the "would-be Crichton" and the "young gentleman" come to expose his impostures. But most important of all, he is also the artist called—who calls himself—to imagine and actually execute this entire scenario.

Poe's Crichton cartoon is a perfect model for the kind of hoaxing that recurs in his work. He has various means for deploying what has been aptly termed his "Rationale of Deception," whose ultimate function is to enlighten rather than to deceive.[8] His resort to hoax, like Dickinson's resort to riddle, is an especially effective device for putting readers to a test of attention. Here his cartoon is itself a hoaxing invitation—a flippant pretense designed to conceal its self-reference by hiding it in plain sight.

As for Coleridge—"a giant in intellect and learning" for Poe—he is also a master of provocative indirection.[9] The title of his *Table-Talk* "deceives us," Poe says (*Marginalia* December 1844, *M* 65), and in his extended eulogium of Coleridge in "Letter to B———" he remarks, quoting the *Biographia Literaria,* that Coleridge "has imprisoned his own conceptions by the barrier he has erected against those of others." While Poe never comments on Coleridge's plagiarisms, his treatment of Coleridge suggests an awareness. Certainly he didn't know that the *Biographia Literaria*'s crucial Chapter X is an elaborate mixture of fact and fiction—a truth about that famous book still unknown to many scholars, including scholars of Romanticism and even of Coleridge. Those English "Jacobin" acquaintances we meet in Chapter X, never identified, were invented by Coleridge to lend a persuasive probability to the biographical structure of his argument.

"Kubla Khan" is an even more arresting case because the famous prose Preface makes such a clear parallel with Poe's equally famous and equally notorious "Philosophy of Composition." Like the English Jacobins of the *Biographia,* Coleridge summoned his "persons from Porlock" for an important expository purpose.[10]

Like the *Biographia*'s Jacobins, they are theoretical fictions created by him to help clarify fundamental truths about poetry and the relation of imagination to the quotidian world.

But what is fiction in Coleridge becomes hoax in Poe and, as a later poet would say (Robert Frost), "that has made all the difference." In the one we have a fiction of Romantic sincerity, in the other a theatre of post-Romantic artifice. The "Central Self" that organizes Romantic self-expression becomes in Poe what Rimbaud called himself, *"un autre,"* one mortal element in a field of social discourse.[11]

That supreme late Romantic Walt Whitman recognized the difference when he said that Poe was one of "the electric lights of imaginative literature, brilliant and dazzling, but with no heat." "The human emotional element . . . passion . . . and personality": these are Whitman's poetic touchstones. But, he says, "We do not see [them] in Edgar Poe."[12] And of course he is correct. Poe summons all of them into his poetry and prose—and many far more exotic and astonishing things—but only to frame them within what Jonathan Elmer has called their "social limit."[13]

Paradoxically, then, the source code that runs Poe's notorious program of art for art's sake is political. In the language of traditional poetics, his work holds up a mirror to a world that appears sunk in illusion. Fear is pervasive. That Poe should himself be judged a victim in and perhaps of that world is the dominant judgment of the biographists. But the most pertinent version of that judgment for understanding Poe's writings is Baudelaire's *poète maudit*.

Crucially, it is not Man who is the cursed victim but the poet as exemplary Man—the defrocked priest of spilt religion, Wordsworth's "Man speaking to Men." As a consequence, the work itself gets pitched past pitch of grief. For now the poetry, the truthful mirror of the world's untruth, no longer stands at a critical distance from its subjects. Nor should its subjects, ourselves, imagine we might stand critically enlightened before the work. As Poe locates his mirror of art within the world it reflects, poetic Enlightenment becomes darkness visible at every point. We were deceived, he tells us, ever to have thought otherwise, as we often have. Poe then invites us to join that revisionary company of the less deceived, who live on living in the cold clarity of their undeceptions.

I am suggesting that an important and neglected ethics and social commentary pervade Poe's work. They are intransigently humanistic and post-theological. Though a special devotion of the poetry, they clearly mark the prose fictions as well, not least masterpieces like "The Fall of the House of Usher" and "Ligeia." We want to remember that each of those tales envelops a poem, "The Haunted Palace" and "The Conqueror Worm," in an imaginative act of commentary. Or perhaps the poems, which were added later, are glossing the tales.

I mean to resist the temptation to consider the fiction here, however, for two reasons. First of all, the social and ethical issues are handled much more nakedly in the poetry and poetics. That such is the case will seem paradoxical since the poetry, unlike that of Poe's major influences Shelley and Byron, studiously avoids taking up social issues directly. The "heresy of *The Didactic*" is one of Poe's signature ideas for a very good reason: in his view, social and ethical attitudes had ossified into various kinds of American ideologies, American exceptionalism and social progress being two of the most baneful. Second, the poetry remains to this day *terra incognita* for many American scholars and teachers. The European view—about as theoretically advanced as you can get—is radically different. But so is the view of American popular culture.

This book takes its point of departure from both of those views. But its argument is directed elsewhere: to readers, especially American readers, who remain uncertain why T. S. Eliot was so "convinced of [Poe's] importance."[14] He explained that judgment—obliquely—in a famous passage in *Little Gidding* (1942):

> So I find words I never thought to speak
> In streets I never thought I should revisit
> When I left my body on a distant shore.
> Since our concern was speech, and speech impelled us
> To purify the dialect of the tribe. (125–129)

Echoing Mallarmé's "Le tombeau d'Edgar Poe" ("Donner un sens plus pur aux mots de la tribu"), Eliot tracks his own poetic purposes back to the distant American shore where Mallarmé discovered Poe's discovery of a new *volgare eloquio* one hundred years before.

Is the passage Eliot's secret confession that Poe had been the feeding source of his own work all along? And that he had to cross the Atlantic to make his American discovery?

Despite what he wrote in *Little Gidding,* Eliot did not solve the puzzle Poe represented. This is especially clear from his persistent critical reflections on Poe, so startlingly candid, as when he wonders, in "From Poe to Valéry," if Poe might all along have been an influence even on his own work ("And yet one cannot be sure that one's own writing has not been influenced by Poe"). At the same time he feels sure enough to say, like Yvor Winters, that Poe's language and thought are "slipshod . . . puerile [and] haphazard." But then too he is "thoroughly convinced of [Poe's] importance," not least because of the "immense" influence Poe has had on the most important and "the most interesting development of poetic consciousness anywhere in [the previous] hundred years" (327, 342). What to do with these contradictions? Because Eliot is uncertain, he ends his last essay on Poe with the words: "I leave it to your consideration." For a critic as severe as Eliot—every bit as severe as the Tomahawk Poe—that sentence explains why his literary reflections hold our attention, even when we might see matters very differently.

If our doors of perception were as open as Eliot's, we might see that Poe also leaves many important and difficult questions for our independent consideration. These questions, for instance: What is the importance of a Modern culture and "poetic consciousness" that, by studying Poe, found its Modern Idiom? How important are other Modern cultures that pursue other idioms? How important is Poe, how important is culture, how important is Modernism? For that matter, how important is poetry itself? And where do we take our bearings: from High Culture, where Poe remains a scandal, or from Popular Culture, where his influence has scarcely diminished?

These are some of the questions I want to raise, if not settle, in this book. They are not questions that press on artists who work in popular media. Poe has had a glorious run in pulp fiction and in film, especially in the experimental freedom of early film, and current graphic fiction is as alive with Poe as he has always been with visual artists from Rossetti and Manet to Odilon Redon, Harry Clarke, and Edmund Dulac.[15] Crises of culture and anxieties of influence do not rule the worlds of children's literature or works that covet the otherwise forbidden realms of the primary imagination. "Otherwise," which is to say wise with the knowledge of forbidden fruit. Those would be God's preserve, as Coleridge told us, and when he ventured there, as he did in "Christabel," he lost his nerve, shrank back, and left us his greatest poem and the truth of its failure. Yvor Winters called it the land of Primitivism and Decadence and warned us all away.[16] That is where Poe, eyes wide shut, went. We go to school and learn to forget what Williams understood: that he actually went there, perhaps before anyone else in America, and that we might go there too.

It is possible to find one's way to that place even with the deceptive maps of scholarship. Or so I believe and so will this book argue.

1

Poe *In Propria Persona*

Cleopatra. It were for me
To throw my sceptre at the injurious gods,
To tell them that this world did equal theirs,
Till they had stol'n our jewel. All's but naught:
Patience is sottish, and impatience does
Become a dog that's mad: then is it sin
To rush into the secret house of death,
Ere death dare come to us?

Shakespeare, *Antony and Cleopatra*
IV. xv. 78–82

The American poet and critic E. C. Stedman once asked Swinburne to give a brief account of himself. Swinburne replied that "knowing as you do the dates and sequence of my published books you know every event of my life."[1] In fact of course a biography of Swinburne's life would hold anyone's interest, though its gravitational field will always be his remarkable literary and cultural career. Poe's life, however, is different—as is clear from the unabating flood of biographical work, popular and scholarly, that keeps trying to wrestle it to earth.

Poe's writings are deeply meshed with his life—more meshed even than Swinburne's, for the brilliant English poet did not spend himself, as Poe did, working in literary trenches, and often in trench warfare. Swinburne fought at Salamis, Poe at Verdun. Poe's life is thus fraught with misery and a chaos of misfortune, more painful exactly because so relentlessly quotidian. As such, his life throws up obstacles to a clear view of the work and its significance, which is very great—as even Eliot was reluctantly forced to insist.[2]

And yet the life, taxed and agitated though it was, must be brought to bear. But if we want a clear view of the work rather than the man—and in particular, of the poetry, which is the focus of this book—we need to step back from the clamor of Poe's driven American world, so energetic and sordid, bound for hope and glory and everywhere bound as well by illusions, lies, betrayals, and self-betrayals.

I say "step back" not to set those matters aside nor to discount their importance, however, as the last section of this study shows.[3] I want to step back to gain a critical perspective that might escape strangulation by the various narratives that have been laid over that legend-laden life. Poe's work, like his life, does not shape itself to that critical form so much in current vogue, a "trajectory." Even his death was, in narrative terms, incoherent.[4] Indeed, biography struggles with his "career" because Poe's life is so bizarre, at once driven and helplessly disordered. Few poets' lives are as painful to read as Poe's.

Those life conditions make a clear view of Poe's work very difficult. The explanatory frameworks that biographers pursue—the many myths of Poe's life—are efforts to discover an order in the extreme disorder of his life and world. In doing this they distract us from the work itself. What is far worse, however, they create an assumption that the work is confused as well: in Lowell's notorious remark, "three-fifths genius and two-fifths sheer fudge."[5] Poe's work thus often comes before us as if it were in desperate need of an enlightened interpreter or the steady hand of critical judgment.

In those circumstances, we want a map for the work that depends less on Poe's life stories and myths, important as they are, than on the life documents that stand behind those narratives. A documentary orientation—the basis of all biography—helps to blunt the pre-emptive interpretational drive that biography, or history for that matter, introduces into any study of cultural materials. It helps to isolate the works as such and so concentrate our critical attention. Paradoxically, the historical importance and originality of Poe's work will, I believe, come into sharper focus as a result. More than that, a documentary approach can help us see that the critical integrity of the work is responding to the territory's discontinuous character. An ordinance survey map is less useful for locating Poe's work in its historical context than a topological space with basins of order shifting under the force of arbitrary and strange attractors. As to such a critical method, the analogy would be to a cubist or action painting or—perhaps even better, given Poe's story-telling interests—to the multiperspectival pictures of an artist like Christopher Derek Bruno.

To that end, I begin with a set of documents of recognized importance. Their chronology is inconsequent to my concerns, except where they show internal revisions. Only slightly less inconsequent, in a general sense, is the order in which these documents will be examined. Not that my arrangement is undeliberate. But I can imagine someone else examining them in a different order, as I can imagine someone else choosing another set, perhaps with some overlaps. My sequence reflects a long struggle to see Poe's poetry steadily and to see it whole. An angel of the odd hovers over Poe's work, not least in the mysteries that leak from and then haunt textual details that often seem too trivial to command close attention. Why does Israfel's music come from "*unusual* strings" (such a pedestrian and colloquial word!), or why is the dream vision of "The Sleeper" located in "the *universal* valley" (my italics)? What did Poe mean when he told James Russell Lowell, "At death the worm is the butterfly"? (Had he written "*becomes* the butterfly" we would have sailed right past that sentence.) Or how does one pronounce "Porphyrogene"? Knowing Poe's conviction that "[a] passionate poem is a contradiction in terms" (*Marginalia* Dec. 1844), what are we to make of Israfel's contempt for "an unimpassioned song"? Or given the explicit theatrical setting of "The Conqueror Worm," did Poe intend to pun with the phrase "condor wings"? And if so, why "condor"? In general, if we say—following Poe's lead—that these texts are meant to be what Poe repeatedly calls "suggestive," is that judgment critically sufficient? And if not, where does the insufficiency lie? In Poe? In us?

I've come to believe that the insufficiency has largely been ours (or mine). What follows is an effort to make it up. The effort is in great part inspired by T. S. Eliot's lifelong struggle to understand what Whitman, radically revising his own earlier negative judgment of Poe, called "Edgar Poe's Significance."[6] Eliot never doubted Poe's enormous cultural significance—how could he, given the importance of Baudelaire, Mallarmé, and Valéry for Eliot's work and view of Modern culture? At the same time, he wondered how anyone could *not* judge the poetry "slipshod," "puerile," and "without perfection in any detail" ("From Poe to Valéry," 327.) He did not himself *make* those judgments; he was joining his voice to an influential line of English and American reading. But his assent left him dissatisfied because he recognized that Poe was the master spirit of an important Modern tradition—for Eliot, the *most* important tradition. I suspect as well that the author of *Old Possum's Book of Practical Cats* (1939) spent a lifetime outgrowing his grey-headed youth.

This study presents an argument for the importance of Poe's poetry *as such*. Making the argument will require that we clarify the relation that issues of "cultural significance" have to issues of language and poetics. The methodology is thus ultimately philological, a critical dimension where close linguistic questions are studied in the context of material and especially documentary culture. In that perspective, Poe's *Marginalia* seems to me the theoretical center of Poe's work.

1. *Marginalia,* November 1844 (*M* 1–4)[7]

In getting my books, I have been always solicitous of an ample margin; this not so much through any love of the thing in itself, however agreeable, as for the facility it affords me of pencilling suggested thoughts, agreements and differences of opinion, or brief critical comments in general. Where what I have to note is too much to be included within the narrow limits of a margin, I commit it to a slip of paper, and deposit it between the leaves; taking care to secure it by an imperceptible portion of gum tragacanth paste.

All this may be whim; it may be not only a very hackneyed, but a very idle practice;—yet I persist in it still; and it affords me pleasure; which is profit, in despite of Mr. Bentham with Mr. Mill on his back.

This making of notes, however, is by no means the making of mere *memoranda*—a custom which has its disadvantages, beyond doubt. *"Ce que je mets sur papier,"* says Bernardin de St. Pierre, *"je remets de ma mémoire, et par consequence je l'oublie;"*—and, in fact, if you wish to forget anything upon the spot, make a note that this thing is to be remembered.

But the purely marginal jottings, done with no eye to the Memorandum Book, have a distinct complexion, and not only a distinct purpose, but none at all; this it is which imparts to them a value. They have a rank somewhat above the chance and desultory comments of literary chit-chat—for these latter are not unfrequently "talk for talk's sake," hurried out of the mouth; while the *marginalia* are deliberately pencilled, because the mind of the reader wishes to unburthen itself of a *thought;*—however flippant—however silly—however trivial—still a thought indeed, not merely a thing that might have been a thought in time, and under more favorable circumstances. In the *marginalia,* too, we talk only to ourselves; we therefore talk freshly—boldly—originally—with *abandonnement*—without conceit—much after the fashion of Jeremy Taylor, and Sir Thomas Browne, and Sir William Temple, and the anatomical Burton, and that most logical analogist, Butler, and some other people of the old day, who were too full of their matter to have any room for their manner, which, being thus left out of question, was a capital manner, indeed,—a model of manners, with a richly marginalic air.

The circumscription of space, too, in these pencillings, has in it something more of advantage than of inconvenience. It compels us (whatever diffuseness of idea we may clandestinely entertain), into Montesquieu-ism, into Tacitus-ism (here I leave out of view the concluding portion of the "Annals")—or even into Carlyle-ism—a thing which, I have been told, is not to be confounded with your ordinary affectation and bad grammar. I say "bad grammar," through sheer obstinacy, because the grammarians (who should know better) insist upon it that I should not. But then grammar is not what these grammarians will have it; and, being merely the analysis of language, with the result of this analysis, must be good or bad just as the analyst is sage or silly—just as he is a Horne Tooke or a Cobbett.

But to our sheep. During a rainy afternoon, not long ago, being in a mood too listless for continuous study, I sought relief from *ennui* in dipping here and there, at random, among the volumes of my library—no very large one, certainly, but sufficiently miscellaneous; and, I flatter myself, not a little *recherché*.

Perhaps it was what the Germans call the "brain-scattering" humor of the moment; but, while the picturesqueness of the numerous pencil-scratches arrested my attention, their helter-skelter-iness of commentary amused me. I found myself at length, forming a wish that it had been some other hand than my own which had so bedevilled the books, and fancying that, in such case, I might have derived no inconsiderable pleasure from turning them over. From this the transition-thought (as Mr. Lyell, or Mr. Murchison, or Mr. Featherstonhaugh would have it) was natural enough:—there might be something even in *my* scribblings which, for the mere sake of scribbling, would have interest for others.

The main difficulty respected the mode of transferring the notes from the volumes—the context from the text—without detriment to that exceedingly frail fabric of intelligibility in which the context was imbedded. With all appliances to boot, with the printed pages at their back, the commentaries were too often like Dodona's oracles—or those of Lycophron Tenebrosus—or the essays of the pedant's pupils, in Quintillian, which were "necessarily excellent, since even he (the pedant) found it impossible to com-

prehend them:"—what, then, would become of it—this context—
if transferred?—if translated? Would it not rather be *traduit*
(traduced) which is the French synonym, or *overzezet* (turned
topsy-turvy) which is the Dutch one?

I concluded, at length, to put extensive faith in the acumen and
imagination of the reader:—this as a general rule. But, in some instances, where even faith would not remove mountains, there
seemed no safer plan than so to re-model the note as to convey
at least the ghost of a conception as to what it was all about. Where,
for such conception, the text itself was absolutely necessary, I could
quote it; where the title of the book commented upon was indispensable, I could name it. In short, like a novel-hero dilemma'd,
I made up my mind "to be guided by circumstances," in default of
more satisfactory rules of conduct.

As for the multitudinous opinion expressed in the subjoined
farrago—as for my present assent to all, or dissent from any portion of it—as to the possibility of my having, in some instances,
altered my mind—or as to the impossibility of my not having altered it often—these are points upon which I say nothing, because
upon these there can be nothing cleverly said. It may be as well to
observe, however, that just as the goodness of your true pun is in
the direct ratio of its intolerability, so is nonsense the essential
sense of the Marginal Note. ❧

This—Poe's first *marginalium*—gives his theoretical justification
for the general marginalian undertaking. At its core is one of
those small and seriously provoking textual events. Distinguish-
ing Marginalia from Memoranda, Poe takes up the former because they have "not only a distinct purpose, but none at all; this
it is that imports to them a value." He goes on to explain the value

of their purposeless purpose by making another distinction: between marginalia and "literary chit-chat." The latter is a form of "talk for talk's sake" whereas with a marginalium "the mind of the reader wishes to unburthen itself of a *thought*." Poe—the writer of this marginalium—exposes the fact that writers are always also readers and, reciprocally, that readers are always rewriting what they read. In that event readers have been provoked to expose themselves, their thinking, to themselves.

That view of the textual event is perhaps the most fundamental nexus for all of Poe's work. Furthermore, the term "unburthen" echoes back to Poe's remark that the "profit" in writing marginalia is a function of the "pleasure" it gives (to hell with Mill and Bentham!). Poe is commenting on the experience of intellectual surprise that marginalia afford: the reader turned spontaneous writer (and talking "only to [himself]") is able to set his thought apart from his act of thinking. He can see it in the objectified context of the physical book that carries it.

Did Poe actually inscribe his books with marginalia? We don't know and probably never will. His library is lost. But the loss helps to clarify the theoretical significance of the *Marginalia,* for this initial foray shows that marginalia for Poe are an imaginative construction, a kind of theory of marginalia. But I say a *kind* of theory because his account does not represent itself as a theory but as a material and factual demonstration: he produces a set of marginalia and then has them printed and distributed. The situation calls attention to another distinctive feature of his work in general: its performative address. The content of his work is regularly made such a codependent function of its form that the two cannot easily be prised apart.

Poe's marginal reflection on marginalia then naturally moves to the question of that objective medium, which he is now able to see in the more comprehensive reader-perspective of the readers of his marginalia. The "context" of the marginalium is crucial and must somehow be preserved since it gives an actual frame to the reading situation. But we now see that the "context" has a doubled and dialectical shape. Something of the initial reading/writing condition must be materially "re-modelled" for the benefit of "the acumen and imagination of the reader" who is reading the marginalium of the initial reader/writer.

The "model" of marginalia is a form designed to accommodate "multitudinous opinion": in the first instance, Poe's own, in the second and correspondent instance, the readers'. The echo of the certainty that Poe's thoughts are open to circumstantial shifts is the equivalent certainty that readers of the marginalia will be left to their own free thoughts. Poe embarks on marginalia with the purpose of engaging those free thoughts, his own and his readers'. The "nonsense" he speaks of at the end is the vertiginous prospect of a cascading fall of marginalia—a fall not unlike the fall of the cascading, dash-driven parataxes that can and will project his energetic prose into a poetical dimension as in *Eureka*.[8]

2. From Poe's review of Hazlitt's *Characters of Shakespeare* (*The Broadway Journal,* August 16, 1845; *ER* 272–273)

In all commentating upon Shakspeare, there has been a radical error, never yet mentioned. It is the error of attempting to expound his characters—to account for their actions—to reconcile his inconsistencies—not as if they were the coinage of a human brain, but as if they had been actual existences upon earth. We talk of Hamlet the man, instead of Hamlet the—dramatis persona—of Hamlet that God, in place of Hamlet that Shakspeare created. If Hamlet had really lived, and if the tragedy were an accurate record of his deeds, from this record (with some trouble) we might, it is true, reconcile his inconsistencies and settle to our satisfaction his true character. But the task becomes the purest absurdity when we deal only with a phantom. It is not (then) the inconsistencies of the acting man which we have as a subject of discussion— (although we proceed as if it were, and thus—inevitably err,) but the whims and vacillations—the conflicting energies and indolences of the poet. It seems to us little less than a miracle, that this obvious point should have been overlooked.

While on this topic, we may as well offer an ill-considered opinion of our own as to the—intention of the poet in the delineation of the Dane. It must have been well known to Shakspeare, that a leading feature in certain more intense classes of intoxication, (from whatever cause,) is an almost irresistible impulse to counterfeit a farther degree of excitement than actually exists. Analogy would lead any thoughtful person to suspect the same impulse in madness—where beyond doubt, it is manifest. This, Shakspeare— felt—not thought. He felt it through his marvellous power of— identification with humanity at large—the ultimate source of his magical influence upon mankind. He wrote of Hamlet as if Hamlet he were; and having, in the first instance, imagined his hero excited to partial insanity by the disclosures of the ghost—he (the poet)—felt that it was natural he should be impelled to exaggerate the insanity. ❧

The corpus of Poe's literary reviews is extensive and famous (or infamous) both for the severity of his judgments and the idiosyncrasy of his interests and literary preferences. Not often enough remarked is the theoretical relation of the reviews to the *Marginalia*. It is well known that equivalent and even verbatim passages appear in both the *Marginalia* and Poe's various reviews, essays, and letters. The critical reflection at the heart of the Hazlitt review, however, has no equivalent text in the *Marginalia*. Nonetheless, the Hazlitt review is striking because it is far less a review of Hazlitt's book than an extended marginalium provoked by Poe's reading of Hazlitt's book: provoked to a reading of Shakespeare and thus provoked to a more general reflection on how poetry works.

Poe's commentary begins as a book review but after its initial paragraph it clearly shifts into a pair of related reflections on poetry, using Shakespeare and *Hamlet* as his exempla. In the first he argues that we miss the poetical importance of Shakespeare if we read his plays—their "actions" and "characters"—"as if they had been actual existences upon earth." Instead, we should read everything as "the coinage of a human brain." The case of Hamlet's "inconsistencies" should not be approached through an appeal to realist criteria of verisimilitude. Rather, they reflect "the conflicting energies and indolences of the poet." The text of the play is a map of the creative mind, a representation of what Keats called "the wreath'd trellis of a working brain" ("Ode to Psyche").

Such a view could well license—has licensed—"biographical readings" of Shakespeare's plays. Poe's commentary is not arguing for such approaches, however, although it is equally true that he would not discountenance them if they were to flaunt their speculative status. His commentary is primarily designed to expose how a complex human being or action gets investigated in a poetical field. Taking Hamlet as a paradigm case of a character deranged from common understanding—his own and ours alike—Poe argues that understanding can be promoted by creating further "counterfeit" forms of derangement—what Eliot would later call "objective correlatives"—by which to reflect on the initial obscurity. Hamlet and *Hamlet* unfold themselves in their further counterfeit forms.[9]

The play *Hamlet* is therefore the dramatic staging of a process of poetic revelation. It is only figuratively a play about a verisimilar man *in extremis,* tangled in a fear- and guilt-ridden world. Shakespeare fashions Hamlet's "intense ... intoxication [and] insanity" not to reflect the condition of Hamlet and his world or even to lift both from their mystified condition. While those representations do transpire, they come as counterfeit images of poetic imagination in action, which itself works by counterfeit images. Because the results of Hamlet's counterfeit theatricals are uniformly terrible, however, a sinister irony haunts Poe's interpretation of the imagination's "marvellous power of—identification with humanity at large." The irony infects Poe's commentary when he remarks on "the conflicting energies and indolences of the poet" who is, it seems, with all his gifts, as unredemptive and unredeemed as the beings with whom, by poetical means, he sympathizes and identifies.

3. From Poe's review of Longfellow's *Ballads and Other Poems, Graham's Magazine* April 1842

In our last number we had some hasty observations on these "Ballads"—observations which we now propose, in some measure, to amplify and explain.

It may be remembered that, among other points, we demurred to Mr. Longfellow's themes, or rather to their general character. We found fault with the too obtrusive nature of their didacticism. Some years ago we urged a similar objection to one or two of the longer pieces of Bryant; and neither time nor reflection has sufficed to modify, in the slightest particular, our convictions upon this topic.

We have said that Mr. Longfellow's conception of the aims of poesy is erroneous; and that thus, laboring at a disadvantage, he does violent wrong to his own high powers; and now the question is, what are his ideas of the aims of the Muse, as we gather these ideas from the general tendency of his poems? It will be at once evident that, imbued with the peculiar spirit of German song (a pure conventionality) he regards the inculcation of a moral as essential. Here we find it necessary to repeat that we have reference only to the general tendency of his compositions; for there are some magnificent exceptions, where, as if by accident, he has permitted his genius to get the better of his conventional prejudice. But didacticism is the prevalent tone of his song. His invention, his imagery, his all, is made subservient to the elucidation of some one or more points (but rarely of more than one) which he looks upon as truth. And that this mode of procedure will find stern defenders should never excite surprise, so long as the world is full to overflowing with cant and conventicles. There are men who will scramble on all fours through the muddiest sloughs of vice to pick up a single apple of virtue. There are things called men who, so long as the sun rolls, will greet with snuffling huzzas every figure that takes upon itself the semblance of truth, even although the figure, in itself only a "stuffed Paddy," be as much out of place as a toga on the statue of Washington, or out of season as rabbits in the days of the dog-star.

Now with as deep a reverence for "the true" as ever inspired the bosom of mortal man, we would limit, in many respects, its modes of inculcation. We would limit to enforce them. We would not render them impotent by dissipation. The demands of truth are severe. She has no sympathy with the myrtles. All that is indispensible in song is all with which she has nothing to do. To deck her in gay robes is to render her a harlot. It is but making her a flaunting paradox to wreathe her in gems and flowers. Even in stating this our present proposition, we verify our own words—we feel the necessity, in enforcing this truth, of descending from metaphor. Let us then be simple and distinct. To convey "the true" we are required to dismiss from the attention all inessentials. We must be perspicuous, precise, terse. We need concentration rather than expansion of mind. We must be calm, unimpassioned, unexcited—in a word, we must be in that peculiar mood which, as nearly as possible, is the exact converse of the poetical. He must be blind indeed who cannot perceive the radical and chasmal difference between the truthful and the poetical modes of inculcation. He must be grossly wedded to conventionalisms who, in spite of this difference, shall still attempt to reconcile the obstinate oils and waters of Poetry and Truth.

Dividing the world of mind into its most obvious and immediately recognisable distinctions, we have the pure intellect, taste, and the moral sense. We place taste between the intellect and the moral sense, because it is just this intermediate space which, in the mind, it occupies. It is the connecting link in the triple chain. It serves to sustain a mutual intelligence between the extremes. It appertains, in strict appreciation, to the former, but is distinguished from the latter by so faint a difference, that Aristotle has not hesitated to class some of its operations among the Virtues themselves.

But the offices of the trio are broadly marked. Just as conscience, or the moral sense, recognises duty; just as the intellect deals with truth; so is it the part of taste alone to inform us of beauty. And Poesy is the handmaiden but of Taste. Yet we would not be misunderstood. This handmaiden is not forbidden to moralise—in her own fashion. She is not forbidden to depict—but to reason and preach, of virtue. As, of this latter, conscience recognises the obligation, so intellect teaches the expediency, while taste contents herself with displaying the beauty: waging war with vice merely on the ground of its inconsistency with fitness, harmony, proportion—in a word with τὸ καλόν.

An important condition of man's immortal nature is thus, plainly, the sense of the Beautiful. This it is which ministers to his delight in the manifold forms and colors and sounds and sentiments amid which he exists. And, just as the eyes of Amaryllis are repeated in the mirror, or the living lily in the lake, so is the mere *record* of these forms and colors and sounds and sentiments—so is their mere oral or written repetition a duplicate source of delight. But this repetition is not Poesy. He who shall merely sing with whatever rapture, in however harmonious strains, or with however vivid a truth of imitation, of the sights and sounds which greet him in common with all mankind—he, we say, has yet failed to prove his divine title. There is still a longing unsatisfied, which he has been impotent to fulfil. There is still a thirst unquenchable, which to allay he has shown us no crystal springs. This burning thirst belongs to the *immortal* essence of man's nature. It is equally a consequence and an indication of his perennial life. It is the desire of the moth for the star. It is not the mere appreciation of the beauty before us. It is a wild effort to reach the beauty above. It is a forethought of the loveliness to come. It is a passion to be satiated by no sub-lunary sights, or sounds, or sentiments, and the soul thus athirst strives to allay its fever in futile efforts at *creation*. Inspired with a prescient ecstasy of the beauty beyond the grave, it struggles by multiform novelty of combination among the things and thoughts of Time, to anticipate some portion of that loveliness whose very elements, perhaps, appertain solely to Eternity. And the result of such effort, on the part of souls fittingly constituted, is alone what mankind have agreed to denominate Poetry.

We say this with little fear of contradiction. Yet the spirit of our assertion must be more heeded than the letter. Mankind have *seemed* to define Poesy in a thousand, and in a thousand conflicting definitions. But the war is one only of words. Induction is as well applicable to this subject as to the most palpable and utilitarian; and by its sober processes we find that, in respect to compositions which have been really received as poems, the *imaginative,* or, more popularly, the creative portions *alone* have ensured them to be so received. Yet these works, on account of these portions, having once been so received and so named, it has happened, naturally and inevitably, that other portions totally unpoetic have not only come to be regarded by the popular voice as poetic, but have been made to serve as false standards of perfection, in the adjustment of other poetical claims. Whatever has been found in whatever has been received as a poem, has been blindly regarded as *ex statû* poetic. And this is a species of gross error which scarcely could have made its way into any less intangible topic. In fact that license which appertains to the Muse herself, it has been thought decorous, if not sagacious to indulge, in all examination of her character.

Poesy is thus seen to be a response—unsatisfactory it is true—but still in some measure a response, to a natural and irrepressible demand. Man being what he is, the time could never have been in which Poesy was not. Its first element is the thirst for supernal Beauty—a beauty which is not afforded the soul by any existing collocation of earth's forms, a beauty which, perhaps, *no possible* combination of these forms would fully produce. Its second element is the attempt to satisfy this thirst by *novel* combinations among those forms of beauty which already exist—or by novel combinations *of those combinations which our predecessors, toiling in chase of the same phantom, have already set in order.* We thus clearly deduce the *novelty,* the *originality,* the *invention,* the *imagination,* or lastly the *creation* of beauty, (for the terms as here employed are synonimous) as the essence of all Poesy. Nor is this idea so much at variance with ordinary opinion as, at first sight, it may appear. A multitude of antique dogmas on this topic will be found, when divested of extrinsic speculation, to be easily resoluble into the definition now proposed. We do nothing more than present tangibly the vague clouds of the world's idea. We recognize the idea itself floating, unsettled, indefinite, in every attempt which has yet been made to circumscribe the conception of "Poesy" in words. A striking instance of this is observable in the fact that no definition exists, in which either "the beautiful," or some one of those qualities which we have above designated synonymously [*sic*] with "creation," has not been pointed out as the *chief* attribute of the Muse. "Invention," however, or "imagination," is by far more commonly insisted upon. The word ποίησις itself (creation) speaks volumes upon this point. Neither will it be amiss here to mention Count Bielfeld's definition of poetry as

"L'art d'exprimer les pensées par la fiction." With this definition (of which the philosophy is profound to a certain extent) the German terms *Dichtkunst,* the art of fiction, and *Dichten,* to feign, which are used for *"poetry"* and *"to make verses,"* are in full and remarkable accordance. It is, nevertheless, in the *combination* of the two omni-prevalent ideas that the novelty and, we believe, the force of our own proposition is to be found.

So far, we have spoken of Poesy as of an abstraction alone. As such, it is obvious that it may be applicable in various moods. The sentiment may develop itself in Sculpture, in Painting, in Music, or otherwise. But our present business is with its development in words—that development to which, in practical acceptation, the world has agreed to limit the term. And at this point there is one consideration which induces us to pause. We cannot make up our minds to admit (as some have admitted) the inessentiality of rhythm. On the contrary, the universality of its use in the earliest poetical efforts of all mankind would be sufficient to assure us, not merely of its congeniality with the Muse, or of its adaptation to her purposes, but of its elementary and indispensible importance. But here we must, perforce, content ourselves with mere suggestion; for this topic is of a character which would lead us too far. We have already spoken of Music as one of the moods of poetical development. It is in Music, perhaps, that the soul most nearly attains that end upon which we have commented—the creation of supernal beauty. It may be, indeed, that this august aim is here even partially or imperfectly attained, *in fact.* The *elements* of that beauty which is felt in sound, *may be* the mutual or common heritage of Earth and Heaven. In the soul's struggles at combination it is thus not impossible that a harp may strike notes not unfamiliar to the angels. And in this view the wonder may well be less that all attempts at defining the character or sentiment of the deeper musical impressions, has been found absolutely futile. Contenting ourselves, therefore, with the firm conviction, that music (in its modifications of rhythm and rhyme) is of so vast a moment in Poesy, as *never* to be neglected by him who is truly poetical—is of so mighty a force in furthering the great aim intended that he is mad who rejects its assistance—content with this idea we shall not pause to maintain its absolute essentiality, for the mere sake of rounding a definition. We will but add, at this point, that the highest possible development of the Poetical Sentiment is to be found in the union of song with music, in its popular sense. The old Bards and Minnesingers possessed, in the fullest perfection, the finest and truest elements of Poesy; and Thomas Moore, singing his own ballads, is but putting the final touch to their completion as poems.

To recapitulate, then, we would define in brief the Poetry of words as the *Rhythmical Creation of Beauty*. Beyond the limits of Beauty its province does not extend. Its sole arbiter is Taste. With the Intellect or with the Conscience it has only collateral relations. It has no dependence, unless incidentally, upon either Duty or *Truth*. That our definition will necessarily exclude much of what, through a supine toleration, has been hitherto ranked as poetical, is a matter which affords us not even momentary concern. We address but the thoughtful, and heed only their approval—with our own. If our suggestions are truthful, then "after many days" shall they be understood as truth, even though found in contradiction of *all* that has been hitherto so understood. If false shall we not be the first to bid them die? ❧

The pertinent section of this document, which is the second installment of Poe's review of Longfellow's 1841 volume, comes in these opening ten paragraphs where he gives an extended explanation of his poetics—that is to say, both his theory of poetry and his view of how it works. The two subjects are for him not only closely related, they are reciprocal. The idea of poetry, its conceptual basis, is not adequately conceivable except as a poetic execution. In this sense the subject of Poe's poetry is always finally the idea of poetry itself, and that idea is only to be realized performatively. Archibald Macleish's well-known remark—itself a poetical performative—is very much to the point: "A poem should not mean/ but be."

The opening paragraphs argue two key points: that the expression of particular ideas—what Poe called "the didactic heresy"—is not the object of poetry and should not be a poet's intention (as it is, Poe avers, Longfellow's); and that, reciprocally, "the rhythmical creation of beauty" is both the poetical object and the poet's intention. A poem thus becomes an object held in view as a problem of how to make the object—understanding the object as a social nexus—an object for an audience. The idea of the poem is its execution—a procedural event fashioned by the poet for a reader's "sentimental," affective response and experience.

Given that understanding, Poe has great difficulty explaining himself in expository prose. These paragraphs are therefore important as a forecast of all the many later prose passages where Poe keeps returning to these same subjects: in the *Marginalia,* in the letters and reviews, most particularly in his three celebrated essays on poetry and poetics, which I shall later be examining in detail. Those expository adventures culminate in *Eureka* where Poe finally discovers a method of strictly poetic exposition, as his subtitle to that work, "A Prose Poem," tells us. The method draws upon what he learned about writing prose as a "magazinist" performer—fiction, nonfiction, and hoax.

These paragraphs also look back to Poe's 1831 "Letter to Mr. ————," the introduction to his 1831 volume *Poems,* where Poe made his first extended effort to lay out his views. The culminant paragraph of that somewhat desultory text is particularly relevant here:

> A poem, in my opinion, is opposed to a work of science by having, for its *immediate* object, pleasure, not truth; to romance, by having for its object an *indefinite* instead of a *definite* pleasure, being a poem only so far as this object is attained; romance presenting perceptible images with definite, poetry with indefinite sensations, to which end music is an *essential,* since the comprehension of sweet sound is our most indefinite conception. Music, when combined with a pleasurable idea, is poetry; music without the idea is simply music; the idea without the music is prose from its very definitiveness. (paragraph 21)

In his various comments and discussions, certain distinctions and critical terms recur. Most important is the close relation of poetry to music, and the "indefinite pleasure" this music-based view of poetry produces. Here and in all the associated documents, Poe insists on the intellectual character of poetic music. It registers as a "conception," very particular in its material expression but "indefinite" in the affect it produces in the reader, as all of Poe's many discussions of poetry and poetics insist. Moreover, by "music" Poe means the network of "sweet sounds" that organize the poetical work.[10] Observe that Poe does not say "Ideas, when combined with pleasurable music, is poetry," but rather the reverse: "Music, when combined with ideas, is poetry." Poe gives the musical resources of a poem intellectual primacy and makes everything else—its semantic features most of all—functions of the music.

A passage in the *Marginalia* of April 1849 (168–169) is also relevant here. Discussing the suggestive "indefinitiveness" of poetical sentiment, Poe says that it is a function of "the conception of sweet sound simply" because the acoustic harmonics of poetry have a conceptual character which is for Poe even more "intellectual," in Shelley's sense, than the concepts of reason or philosophy.

Nor is the term "music" loosely deployed. If, as he argues in his Longfellow review, the "first element [of poetry] is the thirst for supernal BEAUTY . . . Its second element is the attempt to satisfy this thirst by *novel* combinations of those forms of beauty which already exist—or by novel combinations *of combinations which our predecessors . . . have already set in order*" (*ER* 687). The reference is to the acoustic elements of language as they develop through phonemes, syllables, words, phrasal and syntactic units, as well as the host of second-order "combinations" that have been built from those elements by the company of earlier writers and poets. Poe insists on the primacy of music (rather than concept or idea) in order to protect the poetical event from the expository inertia of language itself, which would channel the material resources of language into the abstract regions of what he calls "Truth."

When he plundered his 1842 Longfellow review for the central section of his essay "The Poetic Principle," written some time in 1848, various changes came in, and none more significant than his treatment of the key terms *Truth*, *Passion*, and *Beauty*. In 1842 the great threat to poetical expression comes from "the didactic heresy," and while Poe is careful to argue that poetry "is not forbidden to depict" moral or intellectual ideas, he insists that they be handled formally, as elements contributing to the "harmony" of the composition. Passion, however, remains as a feature of the poet's "wild effort to reach the beauty above"—"a passion," Poe adds, "to be satiated by no sub-lunary sights, or sounds, or sentiments." And Supernal Beauty, though the focus of poetical desire, is inaccessible except as the experience of its failed achievement.

By late 1844 Poe is rethinking the question of poetry and passion. Veering sharply from the Longfellow review where he says that a "calm, unimpassioned" address is "the exact converse of the poetical," he now avers that "poetry and passion are discordant" (*Marginalia* Dec. 1844). The move comes in a discussion of Amelia Welby's poem "The Departed." Welby's work, Poe argues, is "among the class *passionate*," as Longfellow's—"some magnificent exceptions" aside—is among the class didactic.

> True passion is prosaic—homely. Any strong mental emotion stimulates *all* the mental faculties; thus grief the imagination:—but in proportion as the effect is strengthened, the cause surceases. The excited fancy triumphs—the grief is subdued—chastened—is no longer grief. In this mood we are poetic, and it is clear that a poem now written will be poetic in the exact ratio of its dispassion. A passionate poem is a contradiction in terms. When I say, then, that Mrs. Welby's stanzas are good among the class *passionate* (using the term commonly and falsely applied), I mean that her tone is properly subdued. (*M* 61)

Though directed at a specifically elegiac poem, the argument relates to the larger aesthetic question of "satiating" poetry's representation of supernal desires within an order where the desire is experienced but its satisfaction is impossible. Poe seems to have

37

become especially interested in the contradiction the month before, as the following marginalium shows:

> When music affects us to tears, seemingly causeless, we weep *not*, as Gravina supposes, from "excess of pleasure;" but through excess of an impatient, petulant sorrow that, as mere mortals, we are as yet in no condition to banquet upon those supernal ecstasies of which the music affords us merely a suggestive and indefinite glimpse. (*Marginalia* Nov. 1844: M 6)

In the 1842 Longfellow review, that thought was not part of Poe's discussion of poetry as "The desire of the moth for the star." But in 1848 it culminates that celebrated passage from "The Poetic Principle."

In November and December 1844 Poe was working to explain how the dynamic of poetic dispassion operates. The poetic onset of "homely" passion—"impatient, petulant sorrow"—"stimulates *all* the mental faculties" so that "The excited fancy triumphs [and] grief is subdued—chastened." The result is a poetry that reflects in "sublunary" terms what we may imagine as the perfect harmony of "Eternity." For Poe, Mrs. Welby's poem "The Departed" is elegiac, and he instances his own poem "Lenore" as an equivalent work. That he chooses to cite that poem as elegiac, rather than, say, "The Conqueror Worm," draws an important if implicit distinction.

Poe's late 1844 reconsideration of the issue of poetic passion eventually appears when he recasts the 1842 Longfellow review passage in "The Poetic Principle" (1848). The difference between the equivalent 1844 and 1848 passages speaks for itself:

> 1842: There is still a longing unsatisfied, which he has been impotent to fulfill. There is still a thirst unquenchable, which to allay

he has shown us no crystal springs. This burning thirst belongs to the *immortal* essence of man's nature. It is equally a consequence and an indication of his perennial life. It is the desire of the moth for the star. It is not the mere appreciation of the beauty before us. It is a wild effort to reach the beauty above. It is a forethought of the loveliness to come. It is a passion to be satiated by no sublunary sights, or sounds, or sentiments, and the soul thus athirst strives to allay its fever in futile efforts at *creation*. Inspired with a prescient ecstasy of the beauty beyond the grave, it struggles by multiform novelty of combinations among the things and thoughts of Time, to anticipate some portion of that loveliness whose very elements, perhaps, appertain solely to Eternity. And the result of such effort, on the part of souls fittingly constituted, is alone what mankind have agreed to denominate Poetry. (*ER* 685–686)

1848: We have still a thirst unquenchable, to allay which he has not shown us the crystal springs. This thirst belongs to the immortality of Man. It is at once a consequence and an indication of his perennial existence. It is the desire of the moth for the star. It is no mere appreciation of the Beauty before us—but a wild effort to reach the Beauty above. Inspired by an ecstatic prescience of the glories beyond the grave, we struggle, by multiform combinations among the things and thoughts of Time, to attain a portion of that Loveliness whose very elements, perhaps, appertain to eternity alone. And thus when by Poetry—or when by Music, the most entrancing of the Poetic moods—we find ourselves melted into tears—we weep then—not as the Abbaté Gravina supposes—through excess of pleasure, but through a certain, petulant, impatient sorrow at our inability to grasp *now*, wholly, here on earth, at once and for ever, those divine and rapturous joys, of which *through* the poem, or *through* the music, we attain to but brief and indeterminate glimpses. (paragraph 14)

No passage in Poe exposes in a more striking way his departure from certain acknowledged premises of Romantic imagination. Poe has left far behind Keats's Shakespearean dream of negative capability, Coleridge's ideal of poetic "balance and reconciliation," Wordsworth's experience of being "laid asleep in body [to] become a living soul," Byron's Promethean translation of Romantic desire. Instead, he takes as his point of departure the self-deprecating reflection on human love in Shelley's diminished lyric "To ———. [One word is too often profaned.]"

Shelley had recovered a celebrated figure in Eastern poetry—the desire of the moth for the flame—but entirely altered its valence by changing the word "flame" to "star." Forced to assume a Faustian inflection, the eros of personal love mutates to a figure of estrangement. Love becomes a little boy lost in cosmic translation.

> I can give not what men call love,
> > But wilt thou accept not
> The worship the heart lifts above
> > And the Heavens reject not,—
> The desire of the moth for the star,
> > Of the night for the morrow,
> The devotion to something afar
> > From the sphere of our sorrow? (9–16)

Shelley's poem sustains a Romantic Sublime through a striking seizure of affective diminishment, one of his most characteristic poetic moves. Paradoxically, the cosmic orientation that gets fixed in the final two lines emerges from Shelley's initial gesture of self-deprecation.

But when Poe resumes Shelley's figuration, he turns the screw on the idea of an impossible pursuit of creative perfection. The terms "petulant [and] impatient" sink Shelley's devotional gesture to a figure of ordinary, even infantile, frustration. Something perverse and fractious is far more deeply interfused with this poet's life than a capable imagination.[11] The passage thus executes a negative transfiguration of the figure of the poet, a move that may recall for us (as it anticipates in time) both Nietzsche and Rimbaud. Like Nietzsche in *Human All Too Human* (1878), where he forswore his allegiance to the Wagnerian ideal of poetic genius, Poe represented poetic achievement as poetic craftsmanship. That commitment is most elaborately made in his essays "The Philosophy of Composition" and "The Rationale of Verse." Here we see how and why that position is peculiarly cherished because Poe disallows the Shelleyan premise of poetic "inspiration."[12] The poet's limited capabilities are taken for granted. In that respect we also appreciate why the Rimbaud connection is even closer and more important.[13] For Poe's commentary forces us to consider poets as baulked and willful children rather than as pilgrims of eternity. Like Rimbaud, Poe's startling words link the practice of ecstatic poetry—the pursuit of "Supernal Beauty"—to the "âcres hypocrisies" of "L'âme [d'un] enfant livrée aux répugnances" ("Le Poètes de sept ans," 7, 4: "the bitter hypocrisies" in "the soul of a child delivered up to contempt"). We are arrested at this shameless image of a poet of manifestly *incapable* imagination who then sets his cross and captious attitude as the sign of his poetic vocation.

One last change Poe made in 1848 is also important. In 1842 he allows that poetry may introduce moral ideas so long as they are handled "incidentally," by which he means as formal elements within the poem's commitment to musical "harmony, proportion." But he makes no exception for poetry of "the class *passionate*." The exception is removed in 1848:

> the incitements of Passion, or the precepts of Duty, or even the lessons of Truth, may . . . be introduced into a poem, and with advantage; for they may subserve, incidentally, in various ways, the general purposes of the work:—but the true artist will always contrive to tone them down in proper subjection to that *Beauty* which is the atmosphere and the real essence of the poem." (paragraph 34)

4. *Marginalia* November 1844 (*M* 9–10)

All the Bridgewater treatises[14] have failed in noticing *the great* idiosyncrasy in the Divine system of adaptation:—that idiosyncrasy which stamps the adaptation as Divine, in distinction from that which is the work of merely human constructiveness. I speak of the complete *mutuality* of adaptation. For example:—in human constructions, a particular cause has a particular effect—a particular purpose brings about a particular object; but we see no reciprocity. The effect does not re-act upon the cause—the object does not change relations with the purpose. In Divine constructions, the object is either object or purpose, as we choose to regard it, while the purpose is either purpose or object; so that we can never (abstractedly, without concretion—without reference to facts of the moment) decide which is which. For secondary example:—In polar climates, the human frame, to maintain its due caloric, requires, for combustion in the stomach, the most highly ammoniac food, such as train oil. Again:—In polar climates, the sole food afforded man is the oil of abundant seals and whales. Now, whether is oil at hand because imperatively demanded?—or whether is it the only thing demanded because the only thing to be obtained? It is impossible to say. There is an absolute reciprocity of adaptation, for which we seek in vain among the works of man.

The Bridgewater tractists may have avoided this point, on account of its apparent tendency to overthrow the idea of *cause* in general—consequently of a First Cause—of God. But it is more probable that they have failed to perceive what no one preceding them, has, to my knowledge, perceived.

The pleasure which we derive from any exertion of human ingenuity, is in the direct ratio of the *approach* to this species of reciprocity between cause and effect. In the construction of *plot,* for example, in fictitious literature, we should aim at so arranging the points, or incidents, that we cannot distinctly see, in respect to any one of them, whether that one depends from any one other, or upholds it. In this sense, of course, perfection of plot is unattainable *in fact,*—because Man is the constructor. The plots of God are perfect. The Universe is a Plot of God. ❧

Great attention has been paid to this document for the light it sheds on Poe's celebrated theory and method of fictional form and the requirement of a carefully constructed plot. "The universe is a plot of God," Poe observes, and the remark is understandably aligned with Poe's many comments on the need for "unity of effect" in imaginative compositions, prose as well as poetry. His most extensive remarks on the matter come in his 1842 review of Hawthorne's *Twice-Told Tales,* for example: "In the whole composition there should be no word written, of which the tendency, direct or indirect, is not to the one pre-established design" (*ER* 572). This ideal compositional form reflects the artist's pursuit of perfection, "the desire of the moth for the star."

In this marginalium, however, Poe goes further, for he wants to explain the dynamic form of a perfected plot—how it actually functions. Its decisive feature is what he calls "reciprocity." With Babbage's Ninth Bridgewater Treatise most in mind, Poe is deconstructing the traditional idea of the relation between cause and effect, both in general and with respect to imaginative works. In the traditional view "The effect does not react upon the cause," whereas

> In Divine constructions, the object is either object or purpose, as we choose to regard it, while the purpose is either purpose or object; so that we can never (abstractedly, without concretion— without reference to facts of the moment) decide which is which.

So with the construction of plot in literary works, Poe observes that "we should aim at so arranging the points, or incidents, that we cannot distinctly see, in respect to any one of them, whether that one depends from any one other, or upholds it." This perfection of form is the ideal pursuit of all art even though, as he adds, it is "unattainable *in fact,*—because Man is the constructor."

Babbage and the other "Bridgewater tractists" do not recognize this principle of reciprocity, possibly "on account of its apparent tendency to overthrow the idea of *cause* in general—consequently of a First Cause—of God." For Poe, it overthrows neither the idea of cause nor of a First Cause, but it definitely throws both into an entirely new frame of reference.

With respect to imaginative compositions specifically, we can see why Poe told Lowell, in a letter of October 19, 1843, that "Poetry must eschew narrative—except, as you say, dramatically." The problem lies in "the connecting links" that a narrative poem requires, links that inevitably signal a structure organized as a cause/ effect sequence, rather than as a structure of "reciprocities."

"From their very explanatory nature," Poe says, these links must be avoided by *"true poetry*—the highest poetry." He then cites Byron as a poet who sought to overcome this problem of traditional narrative. Byron fractured his narratives into "fragmentary passages, eked out with asterisks"—a move that Poe regards as effective, if also (for him) rather jerry-rigged and inartistic. I note in passing that Byron's method would exfoliate in a host of twentieth-century collage works like *The Waste Land* and *Hugh Selwyn Mauberley*. I also observe (in anticipation) that Poe's poetry itself often works from a structure that is fundamentally collage. "Al Aaraaf" is clearly a collage work.

A month after he published this marginalium, Poe wrote a commentary on the contemporary Romantic narrative *Undine,* where he finds a more artistic management of "the transitions from subject to subject." In the tale, Undine and Bertalda travel together "down the Danube," an event, Poe adds, that would have "tormented" the skill of "An ordinary novelist" to find "a sufficient motive for the voyage." Not so La Motte-Fouqué, who represents the reciprocity of forces at work.

> In this grateful union of friendship and affection winter came and passed away; and spring, with its foliage of tender green, and its heaven of softest blue, succeeded to gladden the hearts of the three inmates of the castle [i.e., Huldbrand, Bertalda, and Undine]. *What wonder, then, that its storks and swallows inspired them also with a disposition to travel?"* (Marginalia December 1844, M 55; Poe's italics)

In a passage not quoted by Poe, La Motte-Fouqué's text itself explicates the reciprocity: "The season was in harmony with their minds, and their minds imparted their own hues to the season."[15] Poe then proceeds to further illustrations of his point:

> How exquisitely artistic is the management of imagination, so visible in the passages where the brooks are water-spirits and the water-spirits brooks—neither distinctly either!

We shall observe that precise kind of effect throughout Poe's poetry. It is not a type of poetic ambiguity or a form of metaphor, however. It is rather a kind of schizoid vision. The relation of the two terms does not work toward their synthesis—Coleridge's theory of poetic symbolism as "the balance and reconciliation of opposite and discordant qualities" (*Biographia Literaria* chapter 14). Poe's effort is to produce texts that further individuate the terms. The result is not a synthesis of the terms but a fission that generates further possible sets of relation—what he called "novel combinations *of combinations.*"

One further comment on this marginalium seems important to make: that Poe calls the universe *a* plot of God, not *the* plot. The remark implies the existence of multiple universes, a thought that *Eureka* will pursue in detail, and where the further implication is also pursued: that the plot(s) of God are conceived by particular human beings, in these cases by Poe. Twice in the *Marginalia* Poe quotes the Baron de Bielfeld approvingly to the effect that one must be God to understand God. Poe's God is created in the image and likeness of Man (*M* 13, 152). Or rather, in the image and likeness of Poe—a distinction of some consequence given the unholy mess of Poe's known life.

Poe's view of God needs clarification. While a very secular view, it nonetheless draws upon the historical emergence of

Christian thought where the humanity of God is the central focus. Poe frequently represents an identity between God and Man, not least at the climax of *Eureka,* and in making that move he draws upon the secular thought of one of his chief influences, Shelley. Both God and Man are figures of creative action, but Poe, like Shelley, focuses on creative action as it appears in a mortal perspective. That is to say, it is action subject to what Shelley called "chance, death, and mutability,

> The clogs of that which else might oversoar
> The loftiest star in unascended heaven,
> Pinnacled dim in the intense inane.
> (*Prometheus Unbound* III. 2. 201–204)

That view drove Poe to take an unusual and highly significant approach to the question of Primary Creation. How "the Universe of Stars" began, for Poe, is strictly speaking unknowable.[16] Because material existence is a fact, however, Poe takes the Deist idea—that an Omnipotent Watchmaker set the clock of Time going—as an assumption that is both necessary and useful. He finds it useful exactly because it allows him to approach the problem as an artistic rather than a theological or philosophical problem. He is strictly speaking not very interested in God, but, like Shelley, he is intensely interested in poetry and its creative function in the mortal world. This leads him to set the syntax and vocabulary of deity at the center of his poetry and poetics. We have no better example of how he does this than in the celebrated theoretical essay "The Philosophy of Composition," where the poet appears as an omnipotent deity with respect to his work.

In this respect we might say that Poe is an atheist, as Shelley declared himself. But he is only an atheist in a very special sense—a sense that is closer to the theist Blake than to the atheist Shelley. The God of philosophy and theology and the traditional churches is for him a multiply dispersed historical reality. Poe is interested in that God and his historical appearances as material for his poetic representations—strictly, as language. The rest is either silence or—as in "Al Aaraaf" and the so-called "angelic dialogues"— a scene where we may watch human beings struggling to understand the nature of human creativity.[17]

5. *Marginalia* March 1846 (*M* 98–101)

Some Frenchman—possibly Montaigne—says: "People talk about thinking, but for my part I never think, except when I sit down to write." It is this never thinking, unless when we sit down to write, which is the cause of so much indifferent composition. But perhaps there is something more involved in the Frenchman's observation than meets the eye. It is certain that the mere act of inditing, tends, in a great degree, to the logicalization of thought. Whenever, on account of its vagueness, I am dissatisfied with a conception of the brain, I resort forthwith to the pen, for the purpose of obtaining, through its aid, the necessary form, consequence and precision.

How very commonly we hear it remarked, that such and such thoughts are beyond the compass of words! I do not believe that any thought, properly so called, is out of the reach of language. I fancy, rather, that where difficulty in expression is experienced, there is, in the intellect which experiences it, a want either of deliberateness or of method. For my own part, I have never had a thought which I could not set down in words, with even more distinctness than that with which I conceived it:—as I have before observed, the thought is logicalized by the effort at (written) expression.

There is, however, a class of fancies, of exquisite delicacy, which are *not* thoughts, and to which, *as yet,* I have found it absolutely impossible to adapt language. I use the word *fancies* at random, and merely because I must use *some* word; but the idea commonly attached to the term is not even remotely applicable to the shadows of shadows in question. They seem to me rather psychal than intellectual. They arise in the soul (alas, how rarely!) only at its epochs of most intense tranquillity—when the bodily and mental health are in perfection—and at those mere points of time where the confines of the waking world blend with those of the world of dreams. I am aware of these "fancies" only when I am upon the very brink of sleep, with the consciousness that I am so. I have satisfied myself that this condition exists but for an inappreciable *point* of time—yet it is crowded with these "shadows of shadows;" and for absolute *thought* there is demanded time's *endurance.*

These "fancies" have in them a pleasurable ecstasy as far beyond the most pleasurable of the world of wakefulness, or of dreams, as the Heaven of the Northman theology is beyond its Hell. I regard the visions, even as they arise, with an awe which, in some measure, moderates or tranquilizes the ecstasy—I so regard them, through a conviction (which seems a portion of the ecstasy itself) that this ecstasy, in itself, is of a character supernal to the Human Nature—is a glimpse of the spirit's outer world; and I arrive at this conclusion—if this term is at all applicable to in-stantaneous intuition—by a perception that the delight experi-enced has, as its element, but *the absoluteness of novelty.* I say the absoluteness—for in these fancies—let me now term them psychal impressions—there is really nothing even approximate in character to impressions ordinarily received. It is as if the five senses were supplanted by five myriad others alien to mortality.

Now, so entire is my faith in the *power of words,* that, at times, I have believed it possible to embody even the evanescence of fancies such as I have attempted to describe. In experiments with this end in view, I have proceeded so far as, first, to control (when the bodily and mental health are good) the existence of the condition:—that is to say, I can now (unless when ill) be sure that the condition will supervene, if I so wish it, at the point of time already described:—of its supervention, until lately, I could never be certain, even under the most favorable circumstances. I mean to say, merely, that now I can be sure, when all circumstances are favorable, of the supervention of the condition, and feel even the capacity of inducing or compelling it:—the favorable circumstances, however, are not the less rare—else had I compelled, already, the Heaven into the Earth.

I have proceeded so far, secondly, as to prevent the lapse from *the point* of which I speak—the point of blending between wakefulness and sleep—as to prevent at will, I say, the lapse from this border-ground into the dominion of sleep. Not that I can *continue* the condition—not that I can render the point more than a point—but that I can startle myself from the point into wakefulness—*and thus transfer the point itself into the realm of Memory*—convey its impressions, or more properly their recollections, to a situation where (although still for a very brief period) I can survey them with the eye of analysis.

For these reasons—that is to say, because I have been enabled to accomplish thus much—I do not altogether despair of embodying in words at least enough of the fancies in question to convey, to certain classes of intellect, a shadowy conception of their character.

In saying this I am not to be understood as supposing that the fancies, or psychal impressions, to which I allude, are confined to my individual self—are not, in a word, common to all mankind—for on this point it is quite impossible that I should form an opinion—but nothing can be more certain than that even a partial record of the impressions would startle the universal intellect of mankind, by the *supremeness of the novelty* of the material employed, and of its consequent suggestions. In a word—should I ever write a paper on this topic, the world will be compelled to acknowledge that, at last, I have done an original thing. ❧

This marginalium addresses one of the central tensions in Poe's work, regularly engaged as the divide separating his critical prose from his poetry, or the "ratiocinative" from the fantastical in his fictional work. Poe recovers that very distinction here: on one hand there is "thinking" and "conception[s] of the brain," on the other "a class of fancies . . . which are *not* thoughts, and to which, *as yet,* I have found it absolutely impossible to adapt language." The problem for Poe is strictly functional: "I do not believe that any thought, properly so called, is out of the reach of language." If "expression" fails, the problem "("I fancy"!) is "a want either of deliberateness or of method." Why then the problem with those "fancies"? Or rather—and this is the purport of the marginalium— what is one to do about it? The answer? Verbalize it. "I fancy" drops casually into Poe's initial ratiocinative discussion only to emerge as the full blown "fancies" of the third paragraph.

Having found a word, however inadequate, for "the shadows of shadows" that he wants to understand and master, he tracks them to their location where he is most "aware" of them: in that hypnagogic region "upon the very brink of sleep." Thus located, the problem they represent becomes more clear: they are fleeting, whereas "for absolute *thought* there is demanded time's *endurance*."

Poe therefore stays with his problem because the problem has now become immediate. It is the problem of carrying the thinking in this very marginalium over to the power of adequate words. As the discussion proceeds his "fancies" become "visions" and "psychal impressions" that produce "a glimpse of the spirit's world." While he does not mention poetry, it is obvious that the language of these fancies is properly the language of poetry as he understands it. But Poe does not shift the discussion to poetry because the problem is a problem of expository prose, as his final sentence avers. Fully executed, the marginalium would become "a paper on this topic." In point of historical fact, Poe would write that paper two years later. He called it *Eureka*.[18]

This marginalium is a kind of prospectus for devising a method to control what Shelley called the "vanishing apparitions that haunt the interlunations of life."[19] "In experiments with this end in view," Poe reports some success in arresting the hypnagogic "*point . . .* between wakefulness and sleep":

> *and thus transfer the point itself into the realm of Memory*—convey its impressions, or more properly their recollections, to a situation where . . . I can survey them with the eye of analysis.

Poe does not say that he wrote up a report on those successful experiments, and we have no record that he did. But here he conveys them into the realm of memory, adding an account to a long history of reports that date back to Aristotle and forward to current research in cognitive psychology. *Eureka* will not be a prospectus or a report. It will be a performative demonstration of "the power of words"[20] to cast fanciful thoughts into a stream of memory where they are thrown open to a reader's experience—initially affective, secondarily analytical.

6. Letter to James Russell Lowell, July 2, 1844

My Dear Mr Lowell,

I can feel for the "constitutional indolence" of which you complain—for it is one of my own besetting sins. I am excessively slothful, and wonderfully industrious—by fits. There are epochs when any kind of mental exercise is torture, and when nothing yields me pleasure but solitary communion with the "mountains & the woods"—the "altars" of Byron. I have thus rambled and dreamed away whole months, and awake, at last, to a sort of mania for composition. Then I scribble all day, and read all night, so long as the disease endures. This is also the temperament of P. P. Cooke, of V the author of "Florence Vane," "Young Rosalie Lee," & some other sweet poems—and I should not be surprised if it were your own. Cooke writes and thinks as you—and I have been told that you resemble him personally.

I am *not* ambitious—unless negatively. I, now and then feel stirred up to excel a fool, merely because I hate to let a fool imagine that he may excel me. Beyond this I feel nothing of ambition. I really perceive that vanity about which most men merely prate—the vanity of the human or temporal life. I live continually in a reverie of the future. I have no faith in human perfectibility. I think that human exertion will have no appreciable effect upon humanity. Man is now only more active—not more happy—nor more wise, than he was 6000 years ago. The result will never vary—and to suppose that it will, is to suppose that the foregone man has lived in vain—that the foregone time is but the rudiment of the future—that the myriads who have perished have not been upon equal footing with ourselves—nor are we with our posterity. I cannot agree to lose sight of man the individual, in man the mass.—I have no belief in spirituality. I think the word a *mere* word. No one has really a conception of spirit. We cannot imagine what is not. We deceive ourselves by the idea of infinitely rarefied matter. Matter escapes the senses by degrees—a stone—a metal—a liquid—the atmosphere—a gas—the luminiferous ether. Beyond this there are other modifications more rare. But to all we attach the notion of a constitution of particles—atomic composition. For this reason only, we think spirit different; for spirit, we say is unparticled, and *therefore is* not matter. But it is clear that if we proceed sufficiently far in our ideas of rarefaction, we shall arrive at a point where the particles coalesce; for, although the particles be infinite, the infinity of littleness in the spaces between them, is an absurdity.—The unparticled matter, permeating & impelling, all things, is God. Its activity is the thought of God—which creates. Man, and other thinking beings, are individualizations of the unparticled matter. Man exists as a "person," by being clothed with matter (the particled matter) which individualizes him. Thus habited, his life is rudimental. What we call "death" is the painful metamorphosis. The stars are the habitations of rudimental beings. But for the necessity of the rudimental life, there would have been no worlds. At death, the worm is the butterfly—still material, but of a matter unrecognized by our organs—recognized, occasionally, perhaps, by the sleep-waker, directly—without organs—through the mesmeric medium. Thus a sleep-waker may see ghosts. Divested of the rudimental covering, the being inhabits *space*—what we suppose to be the immaterial universe—passing every where, and acting all things, by mere volition—cognizant of all secrets but that of the nature of God's volition—the motion, or activity, of the unparticled matter.

You speak of "an estimate of my life"—and, from what I have already said, you will see that I have none to give. I have been too deeply conscious of the mutability and evanescence of temporal things, to give any continuous effort to anything—to be consistent in anything. My life has been *whim*—impulse—passion—a longing for solitude—a scorn of all things present, in an earnest desire for the future.

I am profoundly excited by music, and by some poems—those of Tennyson especially—whom, with Keats, Shelley, Coleridge (occasionally) and a few others of like thought and expression, I regard as the *sole* poets. Music is the perfection of the soul, or idea, of Poetry. The *vagueness* of exultation arous[ed by] a sweet air (which should be strictly indefinite & never too strongly suggestive) is precisely what we should aim at in poetry. Affectation, within bounds, is thus no blemish.

I still adhere to Dickens as either author, or dictator, of the review. My reasons would convince you, could I give them to you—but I have left myself no space. I had two long interviews with Mr D[uyckinck]. when here. Nearly every thing in the critique, I heard from him or suggested to him, personally. The poem of Emerson I read to him.

I have been so negligent as not to preserve copies of any of my volumes of poems—nor was either worthy preservation. The best passages were culled in Hirst's article. I think my best poems, "The Sleeper," "The Conqueror Worm," "The Haunted Palace," <"A Paen"> "Lenore," "Dreamland" & "The Coliseum"—but all have been hurried & unconsidered. My best tales are "Ligeia," The "Gold-Bug," The "Murders in the Rue Morgue," "The Fall of the House of Usher," The "Tell-Tale Heart," The "Black Cat," "William Wilson," & "The Descent into the Maelstrom." "The Purloined Letter," forthcoming in the "Gift," is, perhaps, the best of my tales of ratiocination. I have lately written, for Godey, "The Oblong-Box," and "Thou art the Man"—as yet unpublished. With this, I mail you "The Gold-Bug," which is the only one of my tales I have on hand.

Graham has had, for 9 months, a review of mine on Longfellow's "Spanish Student," which I have "used up," and in which I have exposed some of the grossest plagiarisms ever perpetrated. I can't tell why he does not publish it.—I believe G. intends my Life for the September number, which will be made up by the 10th August. Your article shd be on hand as soon as convenient.

Believe me your true friend.

E A Poe. ❧

No one doubts the significance of this famous letter, and while it is regularly quoted, its three core paragraphs have escaped close analysis. But the letter is as difficult as it is important: it takes a signature and by no means transparent figurative turn; it gives special pertinence to some popular scientific concepts and phenomena, but only in a highly imaginative way; and it deploys two key terms—"rudiment/rudimental" and "affectation"—that require explanation.

Poe opens with a paragraph deploring his fitful and disorderly habits. He is a man constantly swinging between extremes of industry and sloth. He does not mention how "the *rush* of the age" (*Marginalia* Dec. 1846) and its "magazine literature" (*Marginalia* Sept. 1845) have borne upon such a "temperament" because the letter assumes the presence of that context. Indeed, Lowell's preceding letter has already touched on this matter.

But Poe's temperament and condition are not a problem, he says, because "I am *not* ambitious" of worldly success. The remark is not candid. Poe labored hard, often unscrupulously, for financial success and stability, and he died still in pursuit of his most cherished cultural hope: to found and run a periodical of great literary distinction.

If not candid on that matter, however, Poe is ambitious to be as candid and truthful as he can on other and perhaps more important issues.

> I live continually in a reverie of the future. I have no faith in human perfectibility. I think that human exertion will have no appreciable effect upon humanity. Man is now only more active—not more happy—nor more wise, than he was 6000 years ago. The result will never vary—and to suppose that it will, is to suppose that the foregone man has lived in vain—that the foregone time is but the rudiment of the future—that the myriads who have perished have not been upon equal footing with ourselves—nor are we with our posterity. I cannot agree to lose sight of man the individual, in man the mass.—I have no belief in spirituality. I think the word a *mere* word.

The letter takes up three of Poe's most important intellectual preoccupations: the ethical situation of human beings in a mortal world; the conceptual matrix he built for himself to explain the Soul/Body problem—a matrix he himself recognized to be conjectural and fashioned from "a reverie of the future"; and finally, an idea about how poetry ought to be written. As the letter itself suggests, the three topics are closely related.

Poe's view that fundamental human nature has not and will not change over time is crucial. "Foregone" times and persons do not stand in a "rudimentary" relation to later times and persons, and perhaps least of all to times and persons like Poe's own, where progressivist ideas are, Poe thinks, deplorably pervasive. His rejection of moral progress and perfectibility makes him an especially problematic figure in the context of widespread American ideas about the exceptional individual person, on the one hand, and reciprocally, the exceptional historic position—even moral position—of the United States on the other. Whitman's cultural position reflects his commitment to both of those faces of "American Exceptionalism."[21]

Poe is not, however, echoing well-established Christian ideas about the moral depravity of human nature. Though famously contemptuous of what he called "the mob," Poe's antiperfectibilian thought is even more democratic than the ideology and practice of democracy in historical America, as is clear, for instance in a June 1849 marginalium where he distinguishes between a people and a mob. Poe did not see that people in the ancient world were any less (or more) moral or enlightened or intellectually capable than his contemporaries.

Few men were more alert to the human capacity for deception and self-deception, or to the power of human physical needs and desires. But to Poe human illusions and desires fairly define the existential condition of conscious persons living in a material universe. Not only is there no depravity here, the limit condition of human being establishes the divinity proper to human being. For Poe, as for Shelley, God and divinity are human conceptions, though not human conditions except by desire, a desire realized in the execution of "bodily thought."

Poe's thinking here is very close to William Blake's idea that God is a man. Blake saw Jesus as the model of perfect human nature and he expressed it in various ways, for example:

> God Appears & God is Light
> To those poor Souls who dwell in Night
> But does a Human Form Display
> To those who Dwell in Realms of day[22]

That Poe's thought runs along lines very similar to Blake's appears with special clarity in another *Marginalia* from 1849:

> "He that is born to be a man," says Wieland in his "Peregrinus Proteus," "neither should nor can be anything nobler, greater, or better than a man." The fact is, that in efforts to soar above our nature, we invariably fall below it. Your reformist demigods are merely devils turned inside out. (*M* 229)

"Reformist demigods" is of course an antiperfectibilian phrase directed at any number of contemporary political movements, including Abolition. His regular derisive term for such things was Transcendentalism.

Important as that reference is, however, even more striking is how Poe expresses his ethical skepticism, which distinctly recalls famous moments in Blake, such as: "Attempting to be more than

Man We become less."[23] Though not before noticed by either Blake or Poe scholars, the original Wieland passage, translated in 1796, seems to have been the point of reference for both.

In Poe's secular, skeptical humanism, the idea of "spirituality" is materialized. Repeating in a letter to Thomas Holley Chivers a month later much of what he writes here to Lowell, Poe is even more emphatic on the question of a spiritual order. "There is no such thing as spirituality. God is material. All things are material." (To Thomas H. Chivers, July 10, 1844) God is "The unparticled matter, permeating & impelling, all things" into their further "individual- izations of the unparticled matter"—that is, into and as thinking human beings. The equality of God and Man is a logical deduction from such a dynamical model, and the model pervades Poe's work, both theoretical and practical. So for example when Poe reflects critically on the commonplace idea of "moral courage," he objects to a distinction the phrase might imply: "as if there could be cour- age that was *not* moral." The codependence of body and soul or mind and spirit is so fundamental for him that he recommends the phrases "bodily thought" and "muscular imagination" (*Mar- ginalia* June 1849; *M* 195) to express its action.

We want to remember, however, that Poe's argument—if it can be called that—is speculative, as he suggests when he sets his thoughts under the arresting assertion: "I live continually in a rev- erie of the future." By "reverie"—a term that might well character- ize the condition in which all of his poetry operates—Poe means what in "The Sleeper" he calls "conscious slumber" (14). As we have seen, he reflects at length on this *Poe*tic idea in the *Margina- lia* for March 1846. Here it's enough to note the pertinence of the word "future," which figures Poe's awareness of the not-completely- realized state of his speculations.

Not that Poe means to argue a "future" where creative thought could achieve finality. Poe stole Shelley's famous image—"the desire of the moth for the star"—and turned it to a general theory of poetical action, as the phrase "an earnest desire for the future" here indicates. The word "future" is for him a political or historical term only by indirection. It is primarily a verbal image he deploys to transpose the word's chronological reference into spatial terms. So here it designates a determining feature of the geography of poetical pursuit, "whose margin fades," as Tennyson, Poe's other favorite contemporary poet wrote, "for ever and for ever as we move" ("Ulysses").

In fact, figurative discourse organizes what Poe is writing in this letter. Poe's "God" is not a referential descriptor; it is a figure of thought. We are prepared for such a transvaluation of linguistic/ideological values when Poe tells us that he has "no belief in spirituality." His brief accounts of divine and human creative actions/thoughts plainly reshape the known phenomenal world as a dynamic universe created by a god made in the image and likeness of Poe, longing to understand—in his case that means to execute—his own creative desire. Whereas the argument here is severely elliptical, it will get fully elaborated in *Eureka,* as we shall see.[24]

Natural Philosophy and Cosmology supplied Poe with a poetic vocabulary for executing and then reflecting on his thinking, including his thinking about the thinking of others. Hence the pivotal importance of the *Marginalia* in the corpus of his work. The *Marginalia* itself comprises a general—indeed, a *generic*—figure of Poe's commitment to a process of perpetually decentered reflection on the world, which he makes accessible through its discourse fields. Although Poe does not "believe in" God or a supernatural order, he takes very seriously the importance of the discursive field in which both are determinate realities that affect and are affected by action in the historical world.

The third part of the letter's long central paragraph puts Poe's method on full display. Recovering the key word "rudimental" and playing with the words "habited" and "habitations," he sketches a cosmology—again, to be elaborated in detail in *Eureka*—of secular humanism:

> The unparticled matter, permeating & impelling, all things, is God. Its activity is the thought of God—which creates. Man, and other thinking beings, are individualizations of the unparticled matter. Man exists as a "person," by being clothed with matter (the particled matter) which individualizes him. Thus habited, his life is rudimental. What we call "death" is the painful metamorphosis. The stars are the habitations of rudimental beings. But for the necessity of the rudimental life, there would have been no worlds.

The word "God" thus names the primal energy of the material universe. When Poe describes this material creation as "the thought of God," the preposition locates one of Poe's key figures of reciprocity. The universe is imagined simultaneously as the thought that God has and the thought that the material universe has of God. The distinction is at once reciprocal and rudimental.

In either perspective, thinking gets materially dispersed into "Man, and other thinking beings"—that is, into Man and the thinking inhabitants of "the universe of stars." As we know from both "Al Aaraaf" and Poe's celebrated Angelic Dialogues, he found it useful to imagine stars as the "habitations" of angels. And just as God and the universe stand in a reciprocal relation to each other, so too do men and angels. The relation is figured in the echoing words "habited" and "habitations." Human beings, materially "habited," are the "inhabitants" of the material worlds that orbit around their stars. When Poe populates those stars with angelic creatures, he is perpetuating the primal act of creation: the dispersal of materialized thinking. For Poe, committing thought to language—as in this letter—is a deep and complex material event. Poe's angels—"Israfel" for instance—are figures of "other" ranges of thinking that he will use throughout his work as vehicles for investigating transmortal desire in his imaginative works.

The two senses of the words "rudimentary" and "rudimental" define how reciprocity organizes the lifeworld Poe is imagining. Material existence in whatever form is a "basic" and "essential" condition of the lifeworld in all its "particled" forms (OED, first meaning). At the same time, all of those forms are "imperfect" and in some "stage of development or growth" (OED, second meaning). Crucially, Poe is not arguing here that human history has a Hegelian structure—is not contradicting his initial antiprogressivist position. Poe's reciprocal dynamic is strictly confined to the lifeworld of the individual person ("I cannot agree to lose sight of man the individual, in man the mass"). In that conception, he treats "death" as the termination of a person's life in order to explore the moral and psychic import of that event. For Poe, the problem of death is the problem of Death in Life: the individual's experience of irredeemable loss. To locate that personal experience in a more broad or more general context—in the contexts of History or Philosophy, for example—is to lose (or perhaps attempt to flee) the experience of loss. The word "Death" and its discourse field—Poe's favorite territory—can call us back to "the painful metamorphosis."

At death, the worm is the butterfly—still material, but of a matter unrecognized by our organs—recognized, occasionally, perhaps, by the sleep-waker, directly—without organs—through the mesmeric medium. Thus a sleep-waker may see ghosts. Divested of the rudimental covering, the being inhabits *space*—what we suppose to be the immaterial universe—passing every where, and acting all things, by mere volition—cognizant of all secrets but that of the nature of God's volition.

A gloss on his tale "Mesmeric Revelation," this passage keys off its initial remark about the worm and the butterfly. Poe is thinking of the figure traditionally used as an analogy for transmortal passage: the change of state of the caterpillar to the butterfly. In Poe's mesmeric revelation, however, the human being, "Divested of the rudimental covering," enters a transorganic material condition where the rudimentary material transformation (caterpillar to butterfly) succeeds to its metaphysical realization: the identity of those two states of being. The former is a "painful metamorphosis" whereas the latter, being inorganic, is not. The gap between act and the will to act—the temporality of cause and effect—is cancelled, or rather spatially reorganized: "The being inhabits space."

The final paragraph then turns to the practical consequences of these conceptions about poetry. Poe's thought about the musical condition of poetry is spatialized. His keyword, "harmony," represents the unity of effect that "combinations of combinations" build up within a poetic field. When he speaks, as he often does, of the "undercurrent" of meaning that poetry develops, he means this pervasive harmony. In the best poetry, it is present everywhere, though a reader may only engage with it at different moments. His strongest "proof" for this view comes at the beginning of "The Poetic Principle" when he declares that a long poem is a contradiction in terms.

> I am profoundly excited by music, and by some poems—those of Tennyson especially—whom, with Keats, Shelley, Coleridge (occasionally) and a few others of like thought and expression, I regard as the *sole* poets. Music is the perfection of the soul, or idea, of Poetry. The *vagueness* of exultation arous[ed by] a sweet air (which should be strictly indefinite & never too strongly suggestive) is precisely what we should aim at in poetry. Affectation, within bounds, is thus no blemish.

The "sweet air" is the index of the harmony of the composition as a whole: in the words of the *Marginalia* of April 1849, "the conception of sweet sounds simply." Poe's final remark is thus both arresting and deeply pertinent. "Affectation" in poetry—we recognize it principally as "poetic wit"—is the manifestation of artistic effort. He recurs to the matter in a comment on Barrett Browning's poetry:

> The thoughts here belong to a high order of poetry, but could not have been wrought into effective expression, without the aid of those repetitions—those unusual phrases—those *quaintnesses,* in a word, which it has been too long the fashion to censure, indiscriminately, under the one general head of "affectation."
> (*Marginalia* May 1849, *M* 191–192)

Famously deploring Shelley's poetry when it "has a palpable design upon us," Keats made a plea for Romantic sincerity: "if poetry comes not as naturally as the leaves to a tree, it had better not come at all."[25] Sympathizing with both poets, Poe recognizes the importance of a palpable poetic design so long as it isn't a moral or thematic design. It must be the palpable presence of the poem's musical "conception"—a "theme," in a musical sense, "simply."

7. *Marginalia* January 1848 (No. 194) (*M* 150)

If any ambitious man have a fancy to revolutionize, at one effort, the universal world of human thought, human opinion, and human sentiment, the opportunity is his own—the road to immortal renown lies straight, open, and unencumbered before him. All that he has to do is to write and publish a very little book. Its title should be simple—a few plain words—"My Heart Laid Bare." But—this little book must be *true to its title*.

Now, is it not very singular that, with the rabid thirst for notoriety which distinguishes so many of mankind—so many, too, who care not a fig what is thought of them after death, there should not be found one man having sufficient hardihood to write this little book? To *write, I* say. There are ten thousand men who, if the book were once written, would laugh at the notion of being disturbed by its publication during their life, and who could not even conceive *why* they should object to its being published after their death. But to write it—*there is* the rub. No man dare write it. No man ever will dare write it. No man *could* write it, even if he dared. The paper would shrivel and blaze at every touch of the fiery pen. ❧

Reading this now we necessarily read it through Baudelaire, who began writing *Mon Coeur mis à nu* in the early 1860s to test the truth of Poe's challenge. As we know, Baudelaire finally abandoned the work, leaving it behind him unpublished and uncompleted. We may easily imagine that he did this deliberately—or perhaps *fatefully*—in homage to this Sibylline text that set his failed project going, and to the man who charmed him into it. For who *could* look into his heart and publish the whole truth of what he saw there? Bold spirits have imagined such an exploit—Poe did, so did Baudelaire. More blithe spirits—perhaps Sir Philip Sidney—advised poets to do it. It cannot be done, Poe finally declares. Catastrophe will intervene.

Why? We wonder. Thinking of Poe the man, we might surmise that he couldn't face the full truth of his lies, his follies, his plagiarisms, his hypocrisies—all in all, the sum of his failures, which were legion. But that is exactly *not* what this marginalium leads us to consider. However daring or however shameless the person might be, such a book, we are told, is in itself impossible. As impossible as the fulfillment of the desire of the moth for the star.

The force of this marginalium's arresting final sentence hangs upon the mounting rhetoric of the passage. The marginalium is perhaps not exactly the test it appears to be. Poe is clearly playing with his reader, tempting him (definitely him) to take—to imagine he *could* take—an exact measure of himself: his powers, his courage, his ambition, his self-awareness. The tease is also a provocation to move the interested reader—his interest fully engaged by the second paragraph—to imagine, not whether he might possibly make himself more than equal to the ancient challenge to "know thyself," but to make that knowledge public. So the text keeps affecting to wonder, and to keep us wondering, if there might be someone out there (me?) who, having a yen for "immortal renown," would do whatever were necessary to gain it. Poe would surely have remembered that Milton called Fame "the last infirmity of noble minds."

Biographers tell us that Poe can imagine such an intrepid spirit because that sprit is his own imagined self. The judgment seems to me warranted, but its relevance here has less to do with Poe than with the reader Poe's text is calling out. We read this marginalium with an eagerness equal to Poe's perverse intention to call upon that eagerness. Baudelaire took the bait and then, some years later, let it go.

If we meet Poe's perversity with perversity, we might recall here the end of *Song of Myself* and think: Has Poe stopped here ("somewhere," anywhere) waiting for me? Surely he has. And so taking the lead from Baudelaire, we might say to Poe: *Hypocrite scripteur, mon semblable, mon frère.*

That writer/reader reciprocity is one of the thoughts concealed in this riddling text. But the final sentence pushes us to consider that in this impossible quest for truth or fame, one's personal gifts or failings are beside the point. Nor is the daring spirit stopped by some external power. The catastrophe evoked in the final sentence is fearful because it isn't a consummation; it is a beginning, an initiation. The desire of the moth for the star suddenly appears as the desire of the moth for the flame, a figuration Poe, like Shelley, knew through its wide transmission in Persian poetry. But in sharp contrast to that tradition—is Poe transforming it through recollections of Jehovah?—the flame is the agent of its own catastrophic energy. In Persian poetry—even the poetry of Rumi, where the soul's flame has the power to extinguish the candle and the sun itself (rather than vice versa)—the event represents the extinction of the Self and its world of illusions.[26] That event thus brings a promise of unimaginable benevolence, which is the cherished tone of Rumi's poetry.

But in Poe's figuration the agent of desire is not consumed. Poe's fiery finger writes annihilation and having writ, moves on. It is difficult not to think here of the endless "catastrophe" that is the ultimate revelation of *Eureka*.[27]

2

Poetics and Echopoetics

Antony. She is cunning past man's thought.
Enobarbus. Alack, sir, no, her passions are made of nothing but the finest part of pure love. We cannot call her winds and waters sighs and tears; they are greater storms and tempests than almanachs can report. This cannot be cunning in her; if it be, she makes a shower of rain as well as Jove.
Antony. Would I had never seen her!

Shakespeare, *Antony and Cleopatra*
I. ii. 143–150

I

Today Poe's fiercest detractors provide an excellent, perhaps the best, point of departure on his work. This is the case partly because his critics are often distinguished persons, commanding respect—Laura Riding, T. S. Eliot, Yvor Winters.[1] They are useful as well because they press Poe on fundamental issues. In this respect, no single essay on Poe is more important than Winters' "Edgar Allan Poe: A Crisis in the History of American Obscurantism."[2] Focusing on Poe's key theoretical essay "The Poetic Principle," Winters attacks Poe's "obliviousness to the function of intellectual content in poetry" (383). In his preoccupation with beauty, Winters argues, "Poe would rob us of all subject-matter" (385):

> Poe never seems to have grasped the simple and traditional distinction between matter (truth) and manner (beauty); he does not see that beauty is a quality of style, instead of its subject matter, that it is merely the most complete communication possible . . . of the poet's personal realization of a moral (or human) truth . . . that must be understood primarily in conceptual terms, regardless of whether the poem ultimately embodies it in the form of description, narration, or of exposition. (384)

Winters' judgment is a commentary on two of Poe's central ideas about poetry: that it should avoid "the heresy of *The Didactic*" and that its chief object (or "content") is to express the desire "to attain a portion of that Loveliness whose very elements, perhaps, appertain to eternity alone" ("The Poetic Principle," *CT* 198, paragraph 14).

We will want to take the full measure of those ideas, whose import—not least their historical import—is considerable. We can start with some well-known and elementary matters. For Poe, what Winters calls "content"—whether it be conceptual or affective— should not be taken as poetry's expressive goal or "final cause." Winters is mistaken when he asserts that Poe "robs" poetry of content. On the contrary, the "Passion which is the excitement of the Heart" or the "Truth which is the satisfaction of the Reason" are often elements of poetic expression: for "the incitements of Passion, or the precepts of Duty, or even the lessons of Truth, may . . . be introduced into a poem, and with advantage; for they may subserve, incidentally, in various ways, the general purposes of the work" ("The Poetic Principle," *CT* paragraph 18). If through the poetic representation of feeling or thought, Passion or Truth, "we are led to perceive a harmony where none was apparent before," then "the true poetical effect" has been achieved ("The Poetic Principle," *CT* paragraph 34).

The phrase "where none was apparent before" is crucial, for the "harmony" that is Poe's ultimate object of poetry is much more than the sum of the parts of which a poem is composed. This is clear from the passage that sets the key for his essay "The Poetic Principle":

> He who shall simply sing, with however glowing enthusiasm, or with however vivid a truth of description, of the sights, and sounds, and odors, and colors, and sentiments, which greet *him* in common with all mankind—he, I say, has yet failed to prove his divine title. There is still a something in the distance which he has been unable to attain. We have still a thirst unquenchable, to allay which he has not shown us the crystal springs. This thirst belongs to the immortality of Man. It is at once a consequence and an indication of his perennial existence. It is the desire of the moth for the star. It is no mere appreciation of the Beauty before us—but a wild effort to reach the Beauty above.
>
> ("The Poetic Principle," *CT* paragraph 14)

Most important here is the status of that "thirst unquenchable." The poetic presentation of an unattainable object is Poe's limit condition for all poetry. It is not the "harmony" to which a poem has been committed, however. Reason and Passion, Truth and Love—even Uranian Love—"merely [serve] to render the harmony manifest" ("The Poetic Principle," *CT* paragraph 34).[3] The poetic composition succeeds when it has precisely defined the limits that its own materials entail—when (to adapt Matthew Arnold) everything in the poem is to be endured—leaving nothing further to be done.

Poetry can thus only "*show us* the crystal springs" that would quench such a thirst for perfection (my italics). Poe represents that limit condition in musical terms because musical forms resist those conceptual translations that Winters insists upon: "It is in Music, perhaps, that the soul most nearly attains the great end for which, when inspired by the Poetic Sentiment, it struggles— the creation of supernal Beauty" ("The Poetic Principle," *CT* paragraph 16). Again we note the phrasing: "most nearly attains." The object of poetry is harmonic expression. The best poetry produces harmonies that "most nearly attain" the perfect harmony they point toward. Perfect harmony is itself beyond human achievement.

So when Winters speaks of Poe's "helpless inability to separate matter from manner, the poem from its subject" (387), his mistake is felicitous. Poe has no difficulty at all separating matter from manner, as anyone can see in his critical reviews and essays. But the critical ability to draw such distinctions is the reflex of the poetic drive to collapse them into a harmonic composition. The poet is at once gripped by that drive and "helpless" before it. Poe is expressing, in a nineteenth-century dialect, exactly what St. Thomas tells Dante about the cracked mirrors of Nature and Art:

ma la Natura la dà sempre scema,
    similemente operando all' artista,
ch'a l'abito de l'arte ha man che trema. *Paradiso* Canto XIII. 76–78

But nature gives it [perfection] evermore deficient,
    In the like manner working as the artist,
Who has the skill of art and hand that trembles.
(Longfellow translation)

73

So the moral of my story thus far is this: that Poe and Winters hold different theoretical views about what Poe calls "The Poetic Principle." Unsurprisingly, they also differ sharply in their approach to poetic practice and technique. These differences get joined in Winters's brief, dismissive commentary on what he calls Poe's "new system of scansion" (393) as set forth in "The Rationale of Verse." Following that, he subjects a group of Poe's well-known poems to a withering attack. Before reconsidering the rest of Poe's aesthetics or even his poetry directly, we must pause over that essay, Poe's most notorious.

The difficulties of the essay have been apparent to everyone who has worked with it. Consider that it opens by taking the position that "the subject [of prosody] is exceedingly simple . . . and included within the limits of the commonest common sense" ("The Rationale of Verse," *CT* paragraph 2). What follows, however, gives an extended performative lie to that statement. Poe never wrote a longer critical essay, nor anything more tedious and full of convoluted pedantic detail, much of it, as many have noted, close to nonsense—in my view, often deliberated nonsense. In another opening move, at once candid and cunning, so typical of Poe, he remarks that "the clearest subject may be overclouded by mere superabundance of talk." Anyone who sees what is about to come will surely be brought up short by that comment, and even more by the sentences immediately following:

In one case out of a hundred a point is excessively discussed because it is obscure; in the ninety-nine remaining it is obscure because excessively discussed. When a topic is thus circumstanced, the readiest mode of investigating it is to forget that any previous investigation has been attempted.

("The Rationale of Verse," *CT* paragraph 2 3)

74

Is that where he means to leave us when we finish reading *his* essay—to forget that the previous investigation had been undertaken at all?

No one doubts that the essay is full of passages ridiculing both bad verse and—even more—bad versification. Indeed, the essay's central argument is that systems of versification distort one's access to the prosodic effects achieved by successful poetry. That is clearly the point Poe wants to make in his discussion of Byron, the pivotal section of the essay (paragraphs 62–64). The distortion comes because the systems don't—actually, can't—attend to the subtle phonetic effects that good poets, in Poe's judgment, pursue and understand intuitively. Simply, versification cannot explain poetry. But then one wonders: Why write an essay on versification at all? Unlike "The Philosophy of Composition," "The Rationale of Verse" does not succeed in handling that contradiction effectively.

Yet one can see, I think, that it seeks a resolution through satire and comic critique. While its most recent editors, Stuart and Susan Levine, stop short of calling it a hoax, they recognize how one might suspect it a hoax, so "perverse," "slippery," and "sometimes downright funny" (*CT* 77, 79) are its discussions. The problem Poe faces is very like the one he addressed so successfully in "The Philosophy of Composition," which is a brilliant seriocomic performance, at once a satire on the Romantic theory of spontaneous poetic expression and a comic revelation of the imaginative artifice of "The Raven." While examples of the comic and satiric intentions of "The Rationale" can be cited, the essay's critical focus on the pedants of versification has obscured the positive contribution to prosody that he wanted to make.[4]

Poe's critical irony spills into clear view at many points: for example, in his discussion of the verse of Cranch (a "losing" poet) and

Street ("who must be a poet of some eminence, or he will not answer the purpose") (paragraphs 49–56, 80–82); in the ludicrous discussion of "Pease porridge hot" (with its allusion to Cranch (paragraphs 51–52)); and in the passages of verse that Poe constructs in the essay, most notably the final hexameters and the wonderfully impish couplet on mannikin man (paragraphs 99–100, 80–82); or the brief discussion of French verse where we are told, because French verse is measured by syllable rather than by accent, "Therefore, the French have no verse worth the name—which is the fact, put in sufficiently plain terms" (paragraph 91). That is simply a tautological joke, cracked along the same lines as this pleonastic commentary on the nonexistence of the pyrrhic foot:

> Shortness is but the negation of length. To say, then, that two syllables, placed independently of any other syllable, are short, is merely to say that they have no positive length, or enunciation—in other words that they are no syllables—that they do not exist at all. And if, persisting, we add anything about their equality, we are merely floundering in the idea of an identical equation, where, x being equal to x, nothing is shown to be equal to zero. In a word, we can form no conception of a pyrrhic as of an independent foot. It is a mere chimera bred in the mad fancy of a pedant. (paragraph 58)

As so often, Poe hides his satiric intention in plain sight, as when he discusses elisions that prosodists introduce in order to regularize scansion when some particular verse unit does not submit to the scholar's schema:

> But in the case of the terminating m, which is the most readily pronounced of all consonants, (as the infantile *mama* will testify,) and the most impossible to cheat the ear of by any system of slid-

ing—in the case of the *m*, I should be driven to reply that, to the best of my belief, the prosodists did the thing, because they had a fancy for doing it, and wished to see how funny it would look after it was done. (paragraph 87)

Like "The Philosophy of Composition," these critical moves are mock-serious. But even if we recognize them as such, what are we to think when Poe hauls out his own "simple" system (paragraphs 66–73), which seems little more than a prosodic Rube Goldberg machine for scanning complex verse rhythms? At that point and in the related commentaries on Latin poetry, Poe's essay turns so verbose and pedantic that its technical commentaries become unnegotiable. Worse, they prevent access to the true significance of Poe's essay: to expose the phonetic core of poetic expression both ancient and modern (paragraphs 77–83). Poe wrangles with "the gross confusion and antagonism of the scholastic prosody" because of "its marked inapplicability to the reading flow of the rhythms it pretends to illustrate" (paragraph 83). For Poe, when versification tries to take the measure of poetry by marking printed or scripted words, it tends to shift one's attention from the central issue: how the poetry should be sounded.

Critics of "The Rationale of Verse" have pointed out, in a sense quite justly, that because Poe's essay works out a system of scansion that is based on musical notation, it is inapt for scanning his chief object, English poetry. But in a crucial sense the judgment, like Winters's judgment on Poe's lack of content, misses the point of his musical model. The sole purpose of scansion, Poe remarks, is "the distinct marking of the rhythmical, musical, or reading flow. . . . [T]he scansion and the reading flow should go hand in hand" (paragraph 73). Poe is insisting that if poetic verse is to be scanned at all, it should be scanned for oral performance rather than some theoretical verse correctness. Critics of the essay have been distracted from that argument by the outlandish rhetoric Poe deployed to attack and parody systematic versification. Only recently has Poe's true focus been restored by the cognitive psychologist and acoustic-learning scholar Christopher Aruffo, who shows the usefulness of Poe's rationale for marking poetry for oral performance.[5]

In addition to the important practical relevance of Poe's approach, however, his essay also means to sketch what it calls "a philosophy of verse" (paragraph 99). This philosophical intent is grounded in the distinction the essay draws between verse and poetry. For Poe, poetry's versification is the material exponent of its musical aspiration. As he remarks, "it is the triumph of the *physique* over the *morale* of music" (paragraph 21). As such, verse is an artifice that a "cultivated musical taste" uses to mark the musical character of a poetical work. Readers and scholars devise systems of versification to mark the verse devices, the *physique,* of poetry. For their part, poets deploy verse devices to compose works that most closely approximate the complexity of music. That complexity is a relational order based in what Poe calls an "equality of *sounds*" whose minimal unit would be some kind of rhyme or echo, and whose more extensive condition emerges as "melody and harmony." He explains: "In verse, which cannot be better designated than as an inferior or less capable Music, there is, happily, little chance for complexity. Its rigidly simple character not even Science—not even Pedantry can greatly pervert" (paragraph 22). However incapable it may be, poetic versification can be so developed as to index the musical form that is poetry's ultimate, if unreachable, goal. Poe defines that goal as the poetical moment when "[t]he sentiment is [*not*] overwhelmed by the sense" (paragraph 21).

But for Poe, poetic "sentiment" is always under threat of "the sense," and his distinction between these terms is fundamental. Recall the *Marginalia* (April 1849, *M* 167–169) where Poe discusses what he means by poetic sentiment (and what he elsewhere calls the "under current" of poetic expression): that it is a function of "the conception of sweet sound simply" (*M* 168), the intellectual beauty of musical form. "Sense," on the other hand, is a function of the semantic inertia of language. Its clearest threat to sentiment comes as "the didactic heresy," which for Poe represents linguistic "sense" operating in its least "sentimental" or least optative mode. The heresy urges readers to bypass the immediate morphemic and phonetic presence of words in order to traffic instead with their least musical elements, their abstract and/or referred meanings. But even more insidious for Poe is the threat concealed in the very heart of poetic expression: "the inviolable principle of all music" itself, which is *"time"* (paragraph 84). Because learned readers mark time in poetry—sensibly—by that "inferior Music" we call verse, the "rationale of verse"—any rationale, even Poe's—threatens to overwhelm the sentimental spirit's most delicate instrument, music. Consequently, the properly poetical dimension of poetry is experienced as the felt presence of "suggestive" relations and "echos"—those are Poe's typical terms—of fleet phonetic and morphemic forms and their unfolding expansive relations.

II

Poe's musical poetics and its relation to sentimental figurations, while generally understood, remain underexamined, even by his best readers. Richard Fletcher shows how well he understands Poe when he observes that "Hawthorne's symbolism depends on sight, Poe's on sound." Similarly, Charles Feidelson long ago placed Poe squarely in the Symbolist tradition, but in doing so he emphasized the musical rather than the imagistic character of Poe's work: "[Poe] aims at . . . the treatment of meaningful words as though they were autonomous notes of a musical construct, capable of being combined without regard to rational denotation." Reading all of Poe's work through the poetry, Feidelson discounts the referential framework that comes with an imagistic symbolism. In this view, Poe's writing is much closer to Mallarmé's than it is to Baudelaire's,[6] and his closest English counterpart is probably Swinburne, who, like Poe, composed his work with the model of oral performance in mind.[7] These relations tend to be obscured because the intertexts of Mallarmé and Swinburne are both drawn primarily from classical and high cultural archives whereas Poe's are sentimental and popular.

Poe's thinking comes out with greatest clarity in his 1840 discussion of Thomas Moore's poetry, where he argues against Coleridge's distinction between fancy and imagination.[8] The distinction is "unsatisfactory" (*ER* 334) because it proposes a false standard of judgment about degrees of poetical excellence. Imagination and Fancy represent not different *degrees* of poetical expression but different *modes*. So whether a poet is imaginative like Shelley or fanciful like Moore—this is the comparison Poe considers (*ER* 334–337)—does not in itself help to decide the question of excellence.

What makes Moore's fanciful poetry excellent, why is it so superior to Rodman Drake's "puerile," although decidedly "imaginative," verses? To answer that question, Poe uses Shelley's poetry as an especially illuminating case. He starts by dismissing from consideration the poet's chosen "theme" or *"subject"* [Poe's italics] in order to shift the focus from moral ideas to what he calls "moral sentiment." In contrast to Drake, Shelley's poetry transforms its imaginative "conception" into affective form, that is, "the moral sentiments of grace . . . color . . . motion" (*ER* 336–337). "Moral sentiment" is "conception" that has been raised to "the beautiful . . . the ideal" by its translation into a mode that can be primarily accessed through affective rather than cognitive channels.

To explain himself further Poe turns to a musical analogy. Arguing that "there lies beneath the transparent upper current of meaning [in a poem] an under or *suggestive* one," Poe explains their reciprocal operation:

> What we vaguely term the *moral* of any sentiment is its mystic or secondary expression. It has the vast force of an accompaniment in music. This vivifies the air; that spiritualizes the *fanciful* conception, and lifts it into the *ideal*. (*ER* 336–337)

"Meaning" here is entirely musical. Considering the poem as an "air," Poe calls attention to the "accompaniment" that ornaments and vivifies its affective power. The "force" of "This" accompaniment at the "transparent upper current" of the poem produces "that" suggestive undercurrent, lifting the entire composition "into the *ideal*." Crucial to Poe's explanation is the syntax of those three sentences, which short-circuit the referential force of the pronouns "This" and "that" in order to emphasize their reciprocal action.

Working from that set of critical conceptions, we can significantly modify Richard Wilbur's important study of Poe's symbolism. Because Wilbur's poetry owes so much to the Modernist traditions that stress the importance of poetic concretions, he has an acute eye for the imagistic elements in Poe. But his poet's eye betrays his poet's ear. We see this in his excellent if also decidedly incomplete reading of "The Haunted Palace." Wilbur wants to deny the charge brought against Poe—for instance, by Winters—that Poe's poems lack content and are largely "complicated machines for saying 'boo.'"[9] On the contrary, Wilbur says, the paraphernalia of a precise spatialized architecture fairly defines the "frankly and provably allegorical" character of Poe's work. "The Haunted Palace," his set piece example, allows Wilbur to "concentrate" on an "area of Poe's symbolism" (Wilbur 240) that is both manifest and pervasive.

Wilbur points out "what a number of critics have noted, that the poem works off a "comparison between a building and the head of a man" (ibid.) (though it is not exactly the "point by point" comparison he avers). The first four stanzas allegorize "man's mind engaged in harmonious imaginative thought," while the final two "describe the physical and spiritual corruption of the palace and its domain" (Wilbur 240, 241). Wilbur adds that while "Poe does not make it altogether clear *why* one state of mind has given way to another," we can "find the answer" by looking at other works where this fundamental allegory gets deployed. Harmonious imaginative thought gets destroyed when the mind is "invaded by the corrupt and corrupting external world" (Wilbur 242).

But this reading of the poem ignores certain passages that are not only important; they are the poem's most arresting: the strange word "Porphyrogene," for instance, or the startling long-distance rhyme "musically/fantastically," as well as the prosodic oddity of those words. The poem's last two lines fix our attention on a contrast that reaches back across the entire poem. A "hideous" and laughing "throng" raises a "discordant melody" that rhymes darkly with the "troop of Echoes" that in stanza three are "flowing, flowing, flowing" out of the same door as the hideous throng, but in their case singing a perpetual song of "surpassing beauty."

So the poem clearly does work up a symbolic architecture. However, the building does not figure "man's mind," but the poetic mind more specifically, as the poem's musical combinations insist. The distinction is important because, to the degree that a symbolic structure is raised here, its reference is to the dominion of mind in what Poe understood as its supreme musical state. For this reason Poe makes "Porphyrogene" the poem's keyword. Though regularly glossed as an adjective, here it assumes the form of a noun—indeed, a proper noun. This point must be emphasized because, while Poe invented the word, he formed it from his readings in contemporary chemistry and botany, which were generating new proper nouns like oxygen and hydrogen.[10] "Porphyrogene" is in fact both noun and adjective and finally—fundamentally—a synaesthetic figure, both chromatic and phonetic.[11] It is what Poe called, after Champollion, a "phonetic hieroglyph," the most complex of the forms of symbolic figuration.[12] The symbolic building parsed by Wilbur and others houses the real life of this domain, which is far less symbolic than linguistic and, more particularly, phonetic and morphemic: language materialized as a musical architecture.

In this poem Poe is almost certainly replaying the ethical drama he would have read in Tennyson's "The Palace of Art." This is relevant because of the social dysfunction that both poems connect to aesthetic and cultural disease. While this matter will be handled in detail in Chapter 4, I must note here one of Poe's most characteristic and significant poetic moves: to represent the corruption of art in a work of art. His poems regularly stand aside from the convention of first-person Romantic address that they also regularly invoke. To cite the most famous and clear example, the speaker of "The Raven" is not Poe.

The management of "The Haunted Palace" offers a much less dramatic example. In its most celebrated incarnation, the poem is presented as the composition of Roderick Usher and in Usher's story it functions as the image of a tormented mind. But Poe also published it as a free-standing composition under his own name. Nonetheless, even in that form it is not a first-person lyric but a narrative account delivered by some being from an unknown and irreal region, as the opening lines emphasize: "In the greenest of *our* valleys/ By good angels tenanted." Of course one can read the poem as an allegory or index of Poe's mind, as many have. But in that case the homology with Usher raises problems. In a letter of May 29, 1841, Poe told Rufus Griswold that "By the 'Haunted Palace' I mean to imply a mind haunted by phantoms—a disordered brain." Is that brain in a disordered state when it imagines (or inhabits) the "happy valley"—stanzas 1–4—or only later, when ruin comes in stanzas 5–6? The tale tells us that ruin only came later to the original realm of "surpassing beauty."

But the imaginary history recorded by the poem is one thing; the poem itself is another. If the poem's imaginary realm suffers catastrophe—musical concord to musical discord—the imaginative work does not. All of the poem's elements are ultimately concordant: the Sublime and the Beautiful come to make up a new kind of discordant harmony, and the disturbance is all the more pronounced because it is left unexplained. It is only shown, performed as such, and the tale of discord comes primarily to throw that otherwise unimaginable (catastrophic) harmony into relief. Indeed, the poem does not make a mystery of ruination—that comes as a fact of the represented drama. The mystery (and the wonder) is how beauty can be raised in Yeatsian excremental places—indeed, why the putatively "ideal" realm of poetry should turn ruinous.

As Stuart Levine long ago explained, "Catastrophe" for Poe is the supreme figural condition for "the Beauty Effect."[13] Poe's poems typically begin in illusion and end in pain. Most strangely, the musical devices—the verse—that unfold these sentimental conditions equally, as Hopkins might think and Shelley might say, outride their storms on the enchanted boat of a language that always seems obedient to a transmortal command.

Nothing shows the strange music that Poe is pursuing in this poem more than the word "Porphyrogene," as becomes clear when we try to mark its prosody and sound it out. In the largest structural harmony of the poem, the word rhymes with—makes an "equality" with—the sixth lines of the six stanzas, each of which has four syllables (except in the first stanza, a notable because an initial variation that will only be registered as a variation after the fact). The scansion of those lines in three of the six stanzas (the second, fourth, and fifth) seems steadily iambic, although trochaic and spondaic rhythms are so strong throughout the poem, not least in the first of the sixth lines, that a reader necessarily gets mixed prosodic signals, and most of all mixed directions for pronunciation. How one is to speak (or even silently read) the word "Porphyrogene" is a nearly complete mystery.[14] I say nearly because one sound is certain, the sound of "gene." That certainty is important because it tells us that while we may miss a clear understanding of this poem's unheard music—and in particular that *word*'s musical values—we doubt neither its presence nor the poet's deliberate engagement with it. But while Poe has fashioned this strange musical effect, the "ideal" music it "suggests" lies elsewhere and is beyond the power of even the greatest poetry, except "perhaps" in fleeting moments. Prosody makes it accessible, however, as the elusive but definite musical affect of phonetics and morphemics.

III

By 1848 Poe is prepared to declare his musical analogy a "poetic principle": "Music, in its various modes of metre, rhythm, and rhyme, is of so vast a moment in Poetry as never to be wisely rejected" ("The Poetic Principle," *CT* paragraph 16). But having already composed his most ambitious poetical work some months earlier as the "Prose Poem" *Eureka,* he does not insist that the "inferior Music" of verse is indispensable to poetry: "I will not now pause to maintain its absolute essentiality." What is essential is a complex network of "equalities" and "suggestive" relations.

A key moment in the "Rationale" essay comes with the paragraphs that trace, by his admittedly "suppositious progress" (paragraph 36), how a "very considerable . . . amount of complexity" (paragraph 30) can be developed even with the "inferior and less capable Music" of verse. Poe then constructs what he wittily calls a "present *ultimatum* of complexity" (ibid.): a five-line unit of highly artificial verse. As a manifest echo of Tennyson's early poem "Lilian," the lines are a verse model of complex "equality of sound" relations.

> Virginal Lilian, rigidly, humblily dutiful;
> Saintlily, lowlily,
> Thrillingly, holily
> Beautiful!

The allusion to Tennyson is at once pertinent and performative since Tennyson is for Poe the age's supreme poetic music master. Indeed, Poe's recombinant recovery of Tennyson illustrates what Charles Bernstein has recently come to call "Echopoetics."[15] For both, "supernal BEAUTY" has to be pursued "by *novel* combinations among those forms of beauty which already exist—or by novel combinations *of those combinations which our predecessors . . . have already set in order.*" Like Bernstein, Poe is a shameless thief of poetic fire because he wants to make the experience of poetry the subject of his poetry. Both hold to this purpose from their Shelleyan perception that a spiritual vacancy has absorbed the space of the social world

Here we want to concentrate on the technical and theoretical issues, for Poe's parodic invocation of Tennyson is a remarkable piece of argumentative wit. In constructing those four lines of verse Poe is mounting a performative demonstration about the nature of poetry. When, later in the essay, he reorganizes the scansion of the passage from Byron he is doing exactly the same thing. The celebrated opening lines of *The Bride of Abydos* turn in Poe's hands into a passage of rhythmical prose. Indeed, the most breathtaking instance of intellectual brilliance in "The Rationale of Verse" is probably the following, where Poe recalculates "The Conqueror Worm." In order to show how the most advanced kinds of poetry escape "The Narrowness of the limits [of] verse composed of natural feet alone" (*CT* 93), Poe creates an outrageous little couplet in which "There are no *Natural* feet":

/ ◡ ◡   / ◡ ◡   /◡◡ / ◡ ◡   / ◡ ◡
Can it be | fancied that | Deity | ever vin | dictively
/ ◡ ◡   / ◡ ◡   / ◡ ◡   / ◡ ◡ / ◡ ◡
Made in his | image a | mannikin | merely to | madden it?

These are two dactylic lines in which we find natural feet, ("Deity," "mannikin;") feet composed of two words ("fancied that," "image a," "merely to," "madden it;") feet composed of three words ("can it be," "made in his;") a foot composed of a part of a word ("dictively;") and a foot composed of a word and a part of a word ("ever vin"). (*CT* 93)

Note that Poe does not want us to regard any of these constructions as "poetry." In his view they are strictly verse reversionings because, as in "The Philosophy of Composition," he is working here in expository prose, not in poetry. But because the central issues at stake are strictly poetic issues, he forces his own prose towards a performative act of exposition. But its target object is a piece of doggerel verse so impishly suggestive that it acquires real poetic force. We can, indeed we do, imagine that a deity might act so vindictively. At the same time, we can imagine otherwise. But finally what we can actually see are two brilliant lines invented to demonstrate the mankin Poe's power to construct Supreme Fictions, like the fictions of vindictive or benevolent deities, and most especially like this poetic manikin itself.

We shall see how Poe uses these ideas about versification to make poetry in verse. But Poe's most adventurous prose work—for instance "The Philosophy of Composition," much of "The Rationale of Verse," and many of the *Marginalia*—are already working toward the prose-poetic breakthrough that we call *Eureka*. As inheritors of advanced traditions of prose poetry—traditions that Poe himself helped to create—we begin to see here how his prose is poised at any moment to close the gap between the music of poetry and the music of prose. A rationale of doggerel and nonsense poetry is here being worked out, perhaps for the first time, for a poetics of Modernity.

In the case of the Tennyson parody, Poe goes on immediately to explicate its complex if decidedly inferior music: for although it is merely verse, merely parody, it has, like Keats's autumn, its music, too. It is the music of Poe's prose mind. So he has no problem showing, in minute and playfully pedantic detail, that the lines have six types of "absolute equality," two types of "proximate equality," and six types of "proportional equality." Readers following his commentary may well begin to see other possible equalities in the verses. Indeed, Poe validates such thoughts in his next paragraph, where he observes that his fourteenth equality ("the proportional equality, as concerns number, between all the lines, taken collectively, and any individual line—that of four to one"). That culminant equality then "would give birth immediately to the idea of *stanza*," a verse unit that opens the mind to yet another order of equalities that can be built from the inferior music of verse (paragraphs 31–32).

Poe's point is that verse complexities are the visible signs of poetry's aspiration toward supersensible expression. Its inferior music is an important resource for poetry because the sensible measures of verse mark the "struggle to apprehend the supernal Loveliness" ("The Poetic Principle," *CT* paragraph 15). His extended discussion of Byron's *The Bride of Abydos* (paragraphs 60–65) thus serves two critical functions: on one hand, attention to the poem's prosody throws some of Byron's verse imperfections into relief; on the other hand, and far more significantly, it also throws into relief the incompetence of any prosodic analysis, even Poe's, in face of the poetry. To demonstrate his view he translated Byron's verse into unlineated prose. Perhaps thinking of Dr. Johnson's quip about *Paradise Lost* as "verse only to the eye," Poe marks the rhythmical structure of Byron's language so that we can *see* it isn't poetry to be *seen*. It is to be listened to and performatively translated. Byron's "lines will be good" (paragraph 63) whatever system of prosody is thrown at them because their excellence (like their faults) are not a function of versification. For Poe, the simpler the prosodic system the better because the critic will want to follow the lead of the poetic rhythms rather than subject them to a prescriptive verse analysis. I suspect introducing Byron into his essay was a rhetorical move. Poe wanted to set an evidently *poetic* measure for all the other English verses he quotes. In 1848 Byron was still the western world's figural representation of The Poet.

"The Rationale of Verse" is thus a companion piece to "The Poetic Principle," and their connection is important. Together they show that the "poem *per se* ... [the] poem written solely for the poem's sake" ("The Poetic Principle," *CT* paragraph 11) is the focus of Poe's interest. "Content" in Winters's sense serves poetry exactly as versification serves: both are among the compositional elements that poets utilize, part of the *"physique"* in which poetry's "sentiment" or *"morale"*—in decisive contrast to the *moral* element, the poetic "subject" or "theme"—gets incarnated. Clearly the same attitude pervades "The Philosophy of Composition," where Poe sets the compositional elements of "The Raven" as the poem's central subject. But because imaginative hoaxing pervades "The Philosophy of Composition," readers often wonder if Poe actually means what he seems to say about poetic artifice, or is perhaps—as Winters thought—just confused in his thinking. The problem is complicated because hoax plays no part in "The Poetic Principle." The comic and satiric elements in "The Rationale of Verse" certainly recall the ironies that play across "The Philosophy of Composition" but because they are not so well managed, they only rise to successful parody occasionally, and never to full blown imaginative hoax.[16]

These problems get clarified if we reflect on the two ideas that are central to all three essays. One insists that conscious artifice is indispensable to poetry, the other that the actual poetic pursuit—the effort to realize the presence of "Supernal Beauty"—will always expose the limits of conscious artifice. Poe's poetry and poetics both operate under the law of that contradictory and ultimately, as shall see, catastrophic dynamic. His resort to hoax in his most famous essay highlights both the presence and the significance of the dynamic. Hoax is one of the Supreme Fictions of poetic artifice—"supreme" because, like Epic Theatre, it lays bare the heart of its devices, being at once sincere and devious, serious and ironic. To cover a song well-sung by Gertrude Stein, the composition of an aesthetic hoax—in this case, Poe's essay "The Philosophy of Composition"—becomes the explanation of poetic artifice.

When Poe introduces hoax into his aesthetic essay, then, he is discounting the expository authority of its discourse. He makes this move because his subject is *poiesis,* a discursive form that does not easily yield to expository treatment, least of all to definition. A comparison with Coleridge is useful partly because, while both resist a definition of poetry, their different means of avoidance go far to explain the difference between Coleridge's Romantic and Poe's post-Romantic attitude. Poised to define poetry in the *Biographia Literaria* (Chapter XIV), Coleridge deftly slips away from the task, implicitly acknowledging that no definition in the usual sense is possible. The account elaborates Coleridge's justly famous and thoroughly Romantic image of "the poet . . . in ideal perfection."

Like Coleridge, Poe does not attempt to define *poiesis* in "The Philosophy of Composition" but instead takes a similarly functional approach. For Coleridge, that move entails describing how the poet in ideal perfection works. Poe's poet, however, is a thoroughly quotidian character—indeed, a technician, a craftsperson. The satire in the opening paragraphs of his essay ridicules the figure of the vatic poet as a kind of ruse practiced by bad artists to disguise their incompetence. But note that the effect of Poe's functional approach is less to celebrate himself—he makes himself, after all, part of the essay's comic venture—than to insist on the importance of the actual work produced by the poet. By their fruits, not by their ideals, shall you know the poets, and you shall judge their work by its results. Poe's essay has made a sharp turn from a subjective to an objective approach to *poiesis*.

Poe's hoaxing rhetoric is fundamental in this move to objectivity. It implicitly—performatively—argues that the reader has a significant part to play in the work of *poiesis*. The parody establishes a rhetorical frame around "The Raven," its aesthophilosophical commentary, and finally around "Poe" himself, the author of both. All get objectively marked with the sign of unsurmounted contradiction. Reception history then comes to reify the contradiction by showing how readers have been tangled in the coils of the essay. Reaching after fact and reason, readers keep finding themselves in some kind of difficulty. Wise passiveness is out of the question, although another sign of contradiction—a refusal to deal as incisively with Poe's essay as he did in writing it—remains an option. If taken, however, that move will set a reader in the unenviable position of what the essay calls "the literary histrio" (paragraph 5). With respect to aesthetic works, an author cannot be expected to mean what he says. Rather, the author can (and should) mean what he *does*, and, reciprocally, the reader can (and should) see and know what is being done and then make a judgment about how well it was done.

A hoaxing rhetoric brings crisis to any discourse of truth. It is a deliberate move to undermine the verification process that a prose argument implicitly installs through inductive or deductive demonstration, or both. In that respect hoax is primarily a critique of and satire upon the truth pretensions of any expository argument, or what Poe in *Eureka* calls "demonstration": "there is, in this world at least, *no such thing* as demonstration" (*E*, paragraph 4). A parody of a philosophical essay, "The Philosophy of Composition" is more than a parody because the parody is self-reflexive, turned back upon both of its subjects: philosophy (or what Poe calls "theory") and poetic composition. To access the truth-function of such a work you have to negotiate the parodic act itself and not the nominal subjects of the parody. A helpful way to make that move is to read the work not as an essay but as a fiction, a story. In that perspective, "The Philosophy of Composition" will shed its expository and factual character and assume a representational form: composition *as* explanation. The rationale of *poiesis* comes as a performance carried out for attentive readers.

The proper measure of *poiesis* for Poe shifts from sincerity—in commonplace Romantic terms, "the true voice of feeling"—to conscious artifice. So the rhetoric of parody in Poe's essay holds a mirror up to the *poiesis* of "The Raven" and the studied coldness of Poe's poetry in general. Not that intense affect has no place in his poems. On the contrary, both affect and moral concerns come into the poetry but, as we have seen, they come not as meanings but as elements in the poetic, the musical, representation. The impetus to write poetry may be feeling or passion—Wordsworth's "spontaneous overflow," Byron's writing "in red-hot earnest."[17] In both such cases the work unfolds under benevolent signs. "Nature never did betray the heart that loved her," Wordsworth assures us in "Tintern Abbey," and even the last words of Manfred cast a blessing ("Old Man! 'tis not so difficult to die").

With Poe, however, while the impetus to write poetry may be feeling or passion, the compositional event transforms those affects into the objectified presence of what *Eureka* calls the "catastrophe" of the plots of God and of Poe's fallen, godlike poets. Affect is summoned into and then driven from the poems and, like an exorcised demon, set free to enter and take possession of the reader. That poetic moment locates Poe's catastrophe of beauty. It is the moment when a reader understands what Poe is saying: that a thing of beauty—*this* thing of beauty—is not and never can be "a joy forever." That is the ultimate meaning of Poe's mortally immortal word "Nevermore" as well as the sign of the word's pitiless benevolence.

Poe makes this move—his characteristic move—because he sees his enterprising American world emptied of true affect, as if its people were living inside a factitious Romantic poem—a poem by, for instance, Rodman Drake. His poetry does not propose a compensation for the loss of loved and cherished things, it tells a double truth about those losses: first, that they lie beyond redemption; and second, that they need not—indeed, must not—lie beyond a "mournful and never-ending remembrance." For memory is called to cherish even the factitious world.

IV

The work that most fully illustrates and, in illustrating, *explains* Poe's poetics is not one of the prose essays. It is the "Prose Poem" *Eureka*. Given Poe's poetry and poetics, it seems inevitable that he would try to work out a strictly poetic vehicle for representing the theoretical truth of poetry. Prose, the traditional discourse of information and fact, would appear *prima facie* the wrong medium. By contrast, because information and fact are indispensable to the discourse of historical studies and Natural Philosophy—the newly emergent and representative discourses of Poe's world— they were also *prima facie* essential. *Eureka* is grounded in that basic tension.

At one time rarely engaged in a serious way—Valéry's essay being the outstanding exception—*Eureka* has more recently enjoyed a number of important and searching analyses.[18] It is a key document in Poe's poetics because its argument is, like "The Philosophy of Composition," performative rather than expository. Both show that the truth about poetry—its meaning—does not answer to the question "what?" but to the question "how?" Horace's *Ars Poetica* and Pope's *Essay on Criticism* supply much more *truthful* models for a discourse on poetics than Aristotle's *Poetics* or Kant's Third Critique—or, for that matter, than the explanation I am trying to fashion here. Like Horace and Pope, Poe's work assumes that a prosaic exposition will distort poetic truth, tempting readers to make a conceptual rather than an experiential engagement with the issues. He declares *Eureka*'s poetic allegiance at the outset: "I offer this Book of Truths, not in its character of Truth-Teller, but for the Beauty that abounds in its Truth; constituting it true" ("Preface," *E* 5).

"Holding a candle in sunshine" was how Blake saw prosaic and conceptual approaches to works of imagination.[19] The remark throws into relief the difficulty of trying to explain poetry. Carefully parsed, however, it tells us where to hold up our candles: in the prosaic darkness where critics and scholars struggle to improve our collective powers of reflection. Indeed, *Eureka* seems to me, as it has to many others, such an unusual and even such an epochal work that we get furthest with it when we try to lay out the simplest things that we think we know about it.

What makes *Eureka* a poem, then—or let us ask, *how* does its poetry get made? The questions are especially pertinent because Poe's prefatory declaration, like the body of *Eureka,* is written in prose rather than verse. The problem goes deeper than the manifest contradiction in the phrase "Prose Poem." *Eureka* is a work full of declarative facts and information, not least the declaration that it is a prose poem and a Book of Truths. If it is a poem, what is the status of its facticities?

The force of that question gets underscored when we reflect on the two most obvious "poetical" features of *Eureka.* The first is its adherence to "consistency" as the measure of the formal Beauty of its Truth.[20] Because information and facts operate within a correspondence theory of truth, not a coherence theory like Poe's, how *do* those facticities function in *Eureka?* The question becomes more pressing when we reflect upon the engine that generates the "Beauty that abounds" in *Eureka.* Joan Dayan calls the engine "The Analytic of the Dash"; that is, the bibliographical figure that generates the abundant digressions, emendations, transits, and linguistic conversions that comprise the body of the poem. "Presenting a decentered world of unlimited turnings and breakdowns," Dayan observes, "Poe restructures a new space. . . . The dash is [*Eureka's*] sign of extreme capability" (Dayan 64–65). *Eureka* itself gives a different name to this engine: Beauty abounds through the "leap" (paragraph 14) toward second-order facticities, or sets of relations intuitively achieved and then deliberately expressed and elaborated.

In that context, *Eureka* is declaring its allegiance to a mode of poetics that became widespread in the nineteenth century. For European literature and culture, the *fons et origo* of this approach was *Childe Harold's Pilgrimage,* which mapped its poetics to the imaginative representation of Byron's actual travels in the European and Mediterranean world. But the poem is far less a travelogue than it is a performative investigation into the nature of poetry. Tapping the emerging discourses of historicism and ethnography, *Childe Harold's* sweeping historical and geographical facticities developed a new kind of argument for poetry's global relevance. At its core was the Romantic figure of The Poet, the hitherto unacknowledged but now loudly proclaimed legislator of the world because the poet is the master of the world's discursions. The Byronic phenomenon marks Kant and Hegel as the end of the authority of classical philosophy. Romanticism would license imaginative experiments with other literary forms as vehicles for investigating the new master discourses of poetry and poetics: Hoffmann, Hölderlin, Pushkin, Musset, Hugo, Browning, Nerval, Rossetti, and Lautréamont provide notable instances. Coleridge's *Biographia Literaria,* for which Poe had a deep, if also deeply critical, admiration, is especially relevant because its facticities are theological and philosophical—that is to say, ideological. In like manner, Poe's flight of imaginative theory takes off from conceptual facts and scientific information rather than, like Byron's flight, from the circumstantial facts of a lived history.

This entire tradition is important to recall when reading *Eureka*, lest we approach Poe's work as philosophy or, worse yet, as science. It is fundamentally, as Poe said, a "Prose Poem." But it constructs itself around and through the discourse of what was called in the nineteenth century Natural Philosophy—more specifically, a particular and popular region of a nineteenth-century lexicon and methodology. *Eureka* raids the archives of science and cosmology for a language and a syntax that could replace the language and syntax of religion and transcendental philosophy. Susan Manning once shrewdly observed: "The prose [of *Eureka*] simulates the process of mind in the act of self-discovery" (Manning 239).[21] The remark draws our attention to the action rather than the content of the language, an approach that Dayan would brilliantly elaborate a few years later. But when we reflect that Manning's comment might as justly be said of (say) Emerson's essays, we see the need to qualify her insight. For the discourse of science—certainly of Poe's sources in Natural Philosophy—commits itself to proposing nonsubjective processes and discoveries. More accurately perhaps, its processes map to an order that is larger than the poet him or herself, larger even than a poet conceived in Coleridge's "ideal perfection."

A significant index of that encompassing order is the poem's reader, always a prominent player in Poe's work. Paradoxically, the subjective voice of *Eureka*'s poet becomes an equally important index. How the reader and the author function in *Eureka* is strikingly clear in two of the poem's most arresting rhetorical moves. The first comes at the outset with the letter from 2848 found on the *Mare Tenebrarum* of human consciousness.[22] This is Poe's farewell salute to the rhetoric of hoax that he had often found so useful for his work. A critique of contemporary nineteenth-century philosophy and philosophical method, this letter from the future is nonetheless a strictly historical critique whose limited and personal character is emphasized by its double genre (it is an epistle, and it is a parody). We want to remember that while Poe recognizes how different persons exhibit different levels of intellectual and imaginative awareness, he does not recognize an historical progress or ascent of consciousness. Pundit and Pundit's recorder may come from the distant future, but they are still poor forked creatures like everybody else, including Kepler, Mill, and even those maligned eminences whose names Pundit so grotesquely misremembers.

The second rhetorical move is at the end of *Eureka* and comes, once again, as a quotation. In this case, the recorder of *Eureka* reports on the "low voices" of *"Memories"* from some immemorial past. Addressing the reader, the poet says that "I have spoken of *Memories* that haunt us from our Youth [and] pursue us even into our Manhood . . . now and then" (paragraph 265). *Then,* which is also to say *now,* the poet illustrates how these Memories "speak to us with low voices, saying" exactly what is then/now quoted as the last paragraph of *Eureka.* Like the manuscript found in the bottle at the outset, this quotation makes an imaginative figure of objective confrontation. Here the low voices address both the author and the readers of *Eureka* in order to speak of the eternal working of that "Divine Being" in which all creation is here said to participate.

Everything in *Eureka* is thus to be understood as a *saying* or a *speaking,* or—when the poetic figure gets lifted from the physical to the mental order—as a *supposing* or a *fancying* or an *imagining.*

Variations on those projective words control *Eureka*'s discursive representations. They make a harmony with the words *now* and *here*, which mark the opening sentences of more than 20 percent of *Eureka*'s 266 paragraphs, defining the continuing present of the poem's action. Because the core of *Eureka*'s continuously present speakings and supposings comes from the poem's first-person author, the letter from the Future and the voices from the Past are important devices for locating *Eureka*'s first-person in a transtemporal "epoch" named by the ancient Memories "the Night of Time, when a still-existent Being existed" (paragraph 266). As the final paragraph unfolds, we see that the epoch is not measured by Time but by "individual Intelligences"—animal, vegetable, and mineral—that live through "the long succession of ages of consciousness." That phrase, which climaxes the paragraph, plays a cunning game with the English root of the word "succession" and the syntax of its prepositional phrases. The temporality marked in the phrase "long succession *of ages*" (my italics) is undermined when we take the phrase "ages of consciousness" as a nominal phrase modifying "succession." In that perspective, the word "success" gets torqued from the word "succession" in order to expose the difference between "a long succession of ages"—a pure temporality—and "a long succession of ages of consciousness"—a human temporality. (Like the frequently iterated versions of the word "suppose," *Eureka* sports a dazzling set of variations on the word "succession.")

In a nice rhetorical touch that introduces another sign of objectivity into the poem, a footnote gets attached to this portentous paragraph. It calls our attention to a relevant earlier passage (paragraph 187) where *Eureka*'s poet makes a dramatic claim upon supreme intellectual authority. In that case the issue is strictly astronomical: whether, given what is known (and not known) about our particular "Universe of Stars," one may infer the existence of multiple other similar universes ("clusters of clusters" of stars). Carefully laying out the scientific evidence for the existence of multiple universes, Poe shows that such could in fact be the case (paragraphs 180–184). *Eureka* has *in fact* elaborated its possible conception.

But Poe is not interested in making a scientific claim or building a fact-based scientific model that could be tested as a device for making astronomical discoveries: "I am aiming less at physical than at metaphysical order" (paragraph 188). Beyond Poe's model of Cosmos—its second-order facticity—lies his principal object, the Truth of an "impossible conception" (paragraph 185). In paragraph 187 he declares that truth by explaining "By what 'right' a person will 'infer . . . an interminable succession of the "clusters of clusters"'" (paragraph 186):

> I reply that the "right," in a case such as this, depends absolutely on the hardihood of that imagination which ventures to claim the right. Let me declare, only, that, as an individual, I myself feel impelled to the *fancy*—without daring to call it more—that there *does* exist a *limitless* succession of Universes, more or less similar to that of which we have cognizance—to that of which *alone* we shall ever have cognizance—at the very least until the return of our own particular Universe into Unity. *If* such clusters of clusters exist, however—*and they do*—it is abundantly clear that, having had no part in our origin, they have no portion in our laws. They neither attract us, nor we them. Their material—their spirit is not ours—is not that which obtains in any part of our Universe.

They can not impress our senses or our souls. Among them and us—considering all, for the moment, collectively—there are no influences in common. Each exists, apart and independently, *in the bosom of its proper and particular God.* (paragraph 187)

"*If* such clusters of clusters exist, however—*and they do*": that is not the truth of science or philosophy or religion, it is the truth of *poiesis.* It is the power to create not *ex nihilo,* but by consistent extravagance, *ex cathedra.* Recalling Archimedes shouting "Eureka!" as he leapt from his bath, Poe named it the "leap" of an "intuition" that, once taken, laid an obligation upon its agent to bring it to fulfillment—in the present case, to write *Eureka,* whose elaborate series of suppositions and fancies build up a model of a particular universe. *Eureka* becomes one of the possible plots of a god, and its singularity is licensed by the facticities it takes up as its material constraints and *quiddities.* "*Created* by the Volition of . . . the Heart Divine" of a "still existent . . . Divine Being," "this Heart Divine" is revealed, in the fullness of the actual bibliographical time of *Eureka,* as "*our own*" (paragraphs 253–266).

The prefatory paragraphs of *Eureka* (paragraphs 1–6) set out the subject Poe "means to speak of" as well as "the ruling idea" of the poem. The subject is the "*Physical, Metaphysical and Mathematical—of the Material and Spiritual Universe:—of its Essence, its Origin, its Creation, its Present Condition and its Destiny.*" The leading idea is that "*In the Original Unity of the First Thing lies the Secondary Cause of All Things, with the Germ of their Inevitable Annihilation*" [all italics being Poe's]. In reading *Eureka,* both statements should be understood in poetical rather than philosophical or scientific terms. The first statement therefore describes the poem's primary lexicon, the second the poem's view of the rules (the syntax) that order and patrol any deployment of the lexicon. Poe's pronouncement about this *"Material and Spiritual Universe"*— that it is "a plot of God" (paragraph 218)—annotates his poetical understanding of *Eureka*'s materials. Crucially—a fact not observed even by the poem's best readers—Poe's universe is *a* plot of God, not *the* plot. The great truth-telling virtue of poetry, as opposed to philosophy or science, is its ability to expose some metaphysical and metaconceptual truths about the human world by deploying that carefully designed singularity we call "a poem." *Eureka* is *a* model of the Universe—quite like what Charles Saunders Peirce would soon call an "abduction" of that Universe—because, by the law of this human imagination, the Universe should be understood as one, entire, and consistent: a kind of secular translation of the Catholic credal formula "unam, sanctam, catholicam," though Poe might rather have thought, after Horace: "simplex dumtaxat et unum" (*Ars Poetica* 23).

So far as the action of *Eureka* is concerned, then, Poe's "leading idea" gets transformed into an "illustration" of how "an individual impression" of the Universe is possible.

> My general proposition, then, is this:—*In the Original Unity of the First Thing lies the Secondary Cause of All Things, with the Germ of their Inevitable Annihilation.*
>
> In illustration of this idea, I propose to take such a survey of the Universe that the mind may be able really to receive and to perceive an individual impression. (*Eureka* paragraph 6)

Eureka illustrates—enacts—this encompassing mental surveillance for the benefit of "the mind" of the reader. It is an illustration, a model, of how *an* individual mind receives and perceives an impression that is at once individual and total. Two words dominate the organization of *Eureka*'s poetic representation: "now" and, most important of all, "suppose" (in various forms of noun, verb, and adjective). The poetic action is not offered as a discovery but as *the conscious representation* of a discovery process that is already understood. *Childe Harold's Pilgrimage, The Prelude,* "Frost at Midnight," "Ode on a Grecian Urn"—all these are Romantic poems of their first-persons' self-discoveries and, as such, are presented as open-ended, unfinished works with "something evermore about to be" (*The Prelude* VI. 608). Byron's publisher urged him to write more cantos of *Childe Harold,* and *The Prelude* was thus titled—not by the author—because it was exactly that, its further parts having never been completed. The first person of *Eureka,* by contrast, takes the same view of his work as the author of "The Philosophy of Composition" and "The Raven." In the drama of *Eureka,* the speaker's identity with "the action and reaction of the Divine Will" (paragraph 255) emerges to the reader's view as a climactic revelation of a godlike poet whose "Volition" to Supernal Beauty and order is as clear and (pre)determinate as it was to the author of "The Raven."

But *Eureka,* like the Universe, is an entire singularity, *a* poetical model drawn from a particular discourse field. But it unfolds as a singular universe in a Cosmos of other universes, and that larger perspective illuminates the multiple singularities that make up *Eureka*'s special "Universe of Stars."[23] For the poem is as much a summons to other individuals who inhabit *its* particular universe—its readers—as is *Song of Myself.*

This fact appears with special clarity when the model of *Eureka*'s dynamic cycle of "Attraction and Repulsion" has been completely worked out and "Matter" collapses into "absolute Unity" (paragraphs 252–253). Addressing us directly, the poem asks: "are we here to pause?" It then answers itself, that is, it addresses us, its participating agents:

> Not so. On the Universal agglomeration and dissolution, we can readily conceive that a new and perhaps totally different series of conditions may ensue—another creation and radiation, returning into itself—another action and rëaction of the Divine Will. Guiding our imaginations by that omniprevalent law of laws, the law of periodicity, are we not, indeed, more than justified in entertaining a belief—let us say, rather, in indulging a hope—that the processes we have here ventured to contemplate will be renewed forever, and forever, and forever; a novel Universe swelling into existence, and then subsiding into nothingness, at every throb of the Heart Divine?
>
> And now—this Heart Divine—what is it? *It is our own.*
>
> Let not the merely seeming irreverence of this idea frighten our souls from that cool exercise of consciousness—from that deep tranquillity of self-inspection—through which alone we can hope to attain the presence of this, the most sublime of truths, and look it leisurely in the face. (paragaphs 255–257)

Consider the first person plural in this passage. It marks *Eureka* as not just a poem but an oral poem—and *Eureka,* we want to remember, was initially presented as a lecture. A notable feature of the poem's rhetoric is its quietly intimate address: "Not so"; "let us say"; "Let not"; and most arresting of all, "And now—this Heart Divine—what is it? *It is our own.*" The rhetoric appreciates that the revelation may prove startling for some readers, even fearful, but it installs a counter-rhetoric of fearlessness by its pervasive "cool exercise of consciousness." The "most sublime of truths" is more than a justified belief or an indulged hope, it is "now" constituted— in this moment of *fiat lux*—as nonsubjective fact.

Eureka thus works up a theory of Cosmos from the discourse of contemporary Natural Philosophy. But its subject and governing idea, which Poe specified at the outset, are what he elsewhere would call its thematic "upper current." Its thematic "under current" is not a scientific theory; it is a poetic theory. *Eureka* elaborates a detailed model of poetic expression—supposititious, fanciful, and imaginative—out of a discourse field of contemporary prose fact and information. *Eureka*'s nebular model of Cosmos is an objective correlative for a theory of poetry that Poe regards as appropriate to the lingua franca of a post-Enlightenment world.

In assessing *Eureka,* then, it is helpful to recall the important distinction Poe drew (for poems written in rhyme) between verse and poetry. The prose elements in *Eureka*—its facts and information as well as the syntax of their representation—correspond to the versification of rhyming poems, or what "The Rationale of Verse" called their "scientific music" (paragraph 21). Poe judged that contemporary science provided the material means—most particularly, the nebular hypothesis—for representing the fabled Music of the Spheres, the expanding "clusters of clusters" of *Eureka* that correspond to the "novel . . . *combinations of combinations*" (*ER* 687) generated through poetic action.

Eureka is often praised (and dispraised) for its "science," the judgments coming from the perspective of later, more advanced scientific views. While we want to take the exact measure of such historical differences, we should do so in philological terms, just as we take the measure of the differences between the Renaissance discursions of Spenser and the Modernist discursions of Pound. Much as they admired and even imitated Shakespeare, neither Byron nor Keats actually speaks his language, least of all his poetic language. Judging *Eureka*'s success or failure in relation to its "science" is, then, aesthetically mistaken. It violates that fundamental rule laid down by Pope, to begin our readings "in the same spirit that the author writ"—"spirit" clearly signifying what we should now call the discourse field that is actually in play.

Such a philological understanding also makes accessible the discursive features in writers who may seem, as we are wont to say, "in advance of their time." When Poe is judged, as he often is, a "Modernist" or "proto-Modernist" writer, that is the perspective being taken. It registers a commonplace of cultural studies: that every historical moment is pregnant with futurities and that certain writers are their midwives. So readers have seen a forecast of Modernism in the severe formalism of Poe's style. They have also found clear anticipations of a "Big Bang" cosmology in *Eureka,* as well they might since the anticipations are latent possibilities in Poe's contemporary materials.[24] Poe draws them out—*leaps* to them—by his supposititious poetic style. In that move—the poem's most distinctive—*Eureka* makes what may be its most startling forecast: toward the method of scientific discovery Charles Saunders Peirce would soon call and explain as abduction. Hypothesizing an as-yet unrealized truth or conclusion, you test its adequacy by building out a model of greater and greater particularity.[25] You build a dome in air and observe whether it can survive in the environment it requires.

Poe recognizes the *fact* of abduction—what he calls the "intuitive *leap*" (paragraph 14)—in the acts of certain persons like Kepler, but he writes *Eureka* to argue that it can only be properly explained (as opposed to actually executed) by imaginative simulation. *Eureka* is Poe's leap or abduction to the possibility of an explanation of the leap, or what he calls "intuitive" knowledge. It is a simulation/representation of how knowledge and truth are acquired *in fact* by executing the action *in theory,* that is, in poetic imitation. Like Peirce a few years later, Poe is arguing that while deduction and induction are methods for verifying knowledge, they cannot generate new knowledge. Poe dismisses both as "creeping and . . . crawling" (paragraph 21) modes of thought. True knowledge is gained by abductions: imaginative intuitions, guesses, leapings: to recall and reconceive a well-known remark of Keats, by "irritable reachings after fact and reason."[26]

As Peirce would later argue, abduction is the method by which science is able to imagine what it doesn't already know or *think* it knows to be true. Neither Peirce nor any other philosopher (or scientist) could prove or demonstrate the truth of anything we don't already recognize as truth. What we do is abduce recognitions and then submit them to rigorous test. Abduction shows the possibility of a certain state of affairs and, by elaboration of a model, raises or reduces its statistical likelihood. For its part, poetic abduction unfolds in a discourse of imitation, not a discourse of information. As such, its special office is to verify the possibility of the truth of intuition. Insofar as its argument is abductive it implicitly takes the following form: because *Eureka* is a fulfilled model or imitation of the action of intuitive or imaginative knowledge, it expresses the truth of that kind of knowledge in the only way the truth can be expressed: as a representation or performance of the action.

IV. The Catastrophe of Beauty

Of *Eureka*, scholars do not often enough observe that it climaxes at a vision of cosmic "catastrophe" (paragraphs 246–247). The paragraphs that follow the catastrophe (248–266) comprise an imaginative effort to "comprehend" (paragraph 254) and explain it: "But this catastrophe—what is it?" (paragraph 248). Focused on *Eureka*'s postcatastrophic reflections, scholars double down on the problem by dealing almost exclusively with *Eureka*'s final paragraph (266), where "low voices" draw up an explanation of the catastrophe in the language of "an epoch in the Night of Time." As that very phrase suggests, the language of the voices is far removed from the language of Poe's nineteenth century. It is Neo-Platonic and theistic. Poe gains a signal poetic advantage by turning to such a language. It supplies the poem with a discourse that can talk easily—indeed, in terms of the larger purpose of *Eureka*—too easily—about transtemporality. Speaking thus, it flees altogether from the poem's other imperative focus: the "here" and the "now" of what the voices themselves recognize as "a still-existent Being": in mortal terms, a person living in the midst of Eurekan catastrophe (or, even more particularly, Edgar Allan Poe).

Reading *Eureka*'s conclusion primarily through paragraph 266 avoids both its catastrophe—set forth in paragraphs 246–247—and the (so to speak) authorized explanation of the catastrophe, which begins in paragraph 248 and climaxes in paragraph 264. We will get a clearer view of *Eureka* and its poetics, I believe, when we shift our view to those neglected passages.

The catastrophe itself is described in a language passed along to Poe by Kepler, Newton, Humboldt, Laplace, and others he does and does not mention. Since Poe's subject—its "upper current"—is what we would call a moment of cosmological Heat Death, the vision is, if strictly scientific, also apocalyptic:

> Then, indeed, amid unfathomable abysses, will be glaring unimaginable suns. But all this will be merely a climacic magnificence foreboding the great End. Of this End the new genesis described can be but a very partial postponement. While undergoing consolidation, the clusters themselves, with a speed prodigiously accumulative, have been rushing towards their own general centre—and now, with a million-fold electric velocity, commensurate only with their material grandeur and with their spiritual passion for oneness, the majestic remnants of the tribe of Stars flash, at length, into a common embrace. (247)

The "inevitable catastrophe is at hand" (247) in the continuing present *Eureka* has continually insisted upon. It is, however, but *a* moment of "chaotic precipitation, of the moons upon the planets, of the planets upon the suns, and of the suns upon the nuclei." It is only one moment because *Eureka*'s upper current is bearing witness not to the catastrophic death of the Cosmos but of "the Universe of Stars."[27] The Cosmos itself is immortal. The Heat Death of the Universe of Stars is dreadful and terrifying, however, because it is the figure of death that can now both possess and overwhelm the human imagination. The "inevitable catastrophe" is "the great *Now*— the awful Present—the Existing Condition of the Universe" (246).

Shakespeare conjured exactly the same event in a very different language: "I am dying, Egypt, dying" (*Antony and Cleopatra* IV. 15. 23). The congruence leaps from memory to attention when we compare how Antony and Cleopatra characterize Antony's death with how Poe thinks about the death of "the Existing Condition of the Universe." Reflecting on the scientific truth of Universal Catastrophe, Poe calls his readers to take what is essentially a philological view. He begins from the familiar allegorical trope (261–263) about human beings passing from "youth," when a person has no true experience of death, to "manhood," when we "awaken . . . from the truth of [that] dream" (262). At first—Poe is reading in broad historical terms—the shock of the realization leads to a compensatory reaction against the onset of "Doubt, Surprise and Incomprehensibility." *Eureka* then quotes what "They say"—the voices of tradition—to mitigate the fear of death:

> "You live and the time was when you lived not. You have been created. An Intelligence exists greater than your own; and it is only through this Intelligence you live at all." (262)

But Poe *in propria persona* rejects this ancient wisdom: "These things we struggle to comprehend and cannot:—*cannot*, because these things, being untrue, are thus, of necessity, incomprehensible." Why? Because of the fact that

> no one soul *is* inferior to another—that nothing is, or can be, superior to any one soul—that each soul is, in part, its own God—its own Creator:—in a word, that God—the material *and* spiritual God—*now* exists solely in the diffused Matter and Spirit of the Universe. (263)

And that being the case,

> In this view, and in this view alone, we comprehend the riddles of Divine Injustice—of Inexorable Fate. In this view alone the

111

existence of Evil becomes intelligible; but in this view it becomes more—it becomes endurable. Our souls no longer rebel at a *Sorrow* which we ourselves have imposed upon ourselves, in furtherance of our own purposes—with a view—if even with a futile view—to the extension of our own *Joy*. (264)

Upon the factive experience of death, injustice, and evil we impose a "mournful and never-ending remembrance," assuming a burden we choose to bear knowing all the while that the burden is beyond bearing except as an attentive remembrance. Which is as much as to say, in the dialect of Shakespeare:

> *Antony.* Not Caesar's valour hath o'erthrown
>   Antony, But Antony's hath triumph'd on itself.
> *Cleopatra.* So it should be, that none but Antony
>   Should conquer Antony; but woe 'tis so!
> (IV. 15. 19–22)

The catastrophe is not the fact of loss, injustice, and death nor even—in the words of *Eureka*'s final footnote—"the pain of the consideration" of those actual human conditions. For the experience of that pain can be the very emblem of the triumph of a "cool [transmortal] consciousness." But for poetry and poetics, woe 'tis so. Poe has made apocalyptic catastrophe the truth of poetic representations. Poetry—Poe agrees completely with Blake—opens "the doors of perception" so that we might give full attention to The Human Condition within The Poetic Condition, where everything is to be endured but nothing further can be done. From this experience of poetic illusion emerges an irritable reaching after fact and reason that can only be addressed beyond the patrolled borders of poetry, in the living world of politics and ethics.

So conceived, poetry is sometimes called "art for art's sake." Its escapism is its struggle to enter the impossible world of worldly illusions—ideology—and imagine the cost of living in those illusions, which—like one of the best known, The American Dream— appear so beautiful to us that we work daily to perpetuate them. (But woe 'tis so!) For Poe, however, such beauties are always also fearful. Their truth is the Catastrophe their "shadowed eyes remember and foresee."[28]

3

Poetry: or Masks for a Read Death

⟡

Caesar. Make not your thoughts your prisons: no,
   dear queen,
For we intend so to dispose you, as
Yourself shall give us counsel: feed, and sleep. . . .
[*Flourish. Exeunt Caesar and his Train.*]
Cleopatra. He words me girls, he words me, that I
   should not
Be noble to myself. But hark thee Charmian.
[*Whispers Charmian.*]
Iras. Finish, good lady, the bright day is done,
And we are for the dark.

Shakespeare, *Antony and Cleopatra*
V. ii, 184ff.

I

Winters censures Poe's poetry for its lack of content. The charge can seem preposterous in face of Poe's reception history, to which scholars and readers keep adding further suggestions about the poetry's sources, references, and meanings. And yet in an important sense Winters is correct, as that reception history shows, for the language of the poems is not precisely defining but precisely suggestive.

The style works to unhinge both words and syntax from semantic certainty. That is the glory and the nothing of it. The poems illustrate themselves and in that respect resemble the demonstrations of mathematical theorems. So we rightly say that they are performative rather than expressive. They are organized not by symbolic form but by cumulative associations. As with Rimbaud, who studied and admired Poe, their images do not refer, they resonate.

A nice example of Poe's method comes as the opening stanza of "To Helen," a notable crux in his work:

> Helen, thy beauty is to me
> > Like those Nicéan barks of yore,
> That gently, o'er a perfumed sea,
> > The weary way-worn wanderer bore
> > To his own native shore.

We need go no further than Mabbott's extensive notes to see how the key nominals in the passage have been objects of obsessive inquiry and search.[1] The result is not a consensus about their referents but an array of alternatives. Taken together these commentaries become a complex sign of the poem's associational resonance. In that sense, we see the pertinence of James Russell Lowell's remark that Poe's poem "is like a Greek column, because of its perfection." The point is not whether the poem is in fact "perfect," but that it suggests the idea of perfection by making itself its own subject: "this poem written solely for the poem's sake." Addressed "To Helen," the poem is also and at once a journey *to* Helen and to her Hellenic world, as well as the means by which the journey is accomplished.[2] Pressed further, as the poem's complex and problematic resonances invite us to do, that "content" betrays the

dark metastasis that Poe called its "under current of meaning"—
"mournful and never ending remembrance."

Writing poetry in this way turns Poe's poems into a set of demonstrative arguments about poetry itself—more precisely, about Poe's theory of poetry. In his most ambitious poetical work, *Eureka,* he denied that his poetical method—confessedly subjective and imaginative—ought to be called a method of demonstration. His view follows from his commitment to argument by imaginative conceivability (abduction as opposed to inductive or deductive "demonstration"). It has much in common with Blake's view of poetical imagination, as well as with Keats's thought that "what the *Imagination* seizes as beauty must be Truth, *whether it existed before or not.*" In this context, Stein's theory of "Composition as Explanation" is perhaps the most appropriate way of understanding Poe's poetics.[3]

His theory is important because it breaks so sharply with tradition. It is neither an ontological nor a psychological theory, both of which, for example, are seriously pursued in Coleridge's *Biographia Literaria.*[4] Poe's theory is procedural: to know what poetry is you want to observe how it works, and you only achieve that if, like a scientist investigating electricity, you experiment with its actual resources and possibilities. From that vantage, everything about the poem will appear to be handled impersonally, including the poet him or herself. We observe this quest for impersonality in one of the most notable features of Poe's poetry: its tendency to objectify a poem's first-person address. Although the situation resembles the procedure of a dramatic monologue, ultimately it is very different.[5]

After the early "Tamerlane," Poe does not again deploy dramatic monologue; that is, he does not put the words of his poems in the mouths of public speakers, whether historical or literary.[6] But the traditional dramatic monologue wants those referential contexts—historical or intertextual—to shape our sense of what the poem means. "Tamerlane" itself does anticipate Poe's normal procedure because it is *not* Tamerlane whom Poe ventriloquizes but Byron, as is apparent from the poem's clear source, the famous last words of the Giaour in Byron's celebrated poem.

Poe's mature poems, however, are not voiced by people—not even by poets like Byron—but by highly imaginative and anonymous characters. The irreal settings of Poe's poems mark the character of the speakers, though only "Israfel," "The Raven," and "Lenore" explicitly identify them as (anonymous) writers and poets. "The Raven" and its prose exegesis, "The Philosophy of Composition," put the logic of Poe's design on complete display. Poe dons the mask of a poet-craftsman who has constructed the text in which we observe the spontaneous overflows of an unselfconscious writer tormented by a loss he does not want to remember. While the essay calls our attention to the distinction the poem draws between writer and writer, the poem hides it in plain sight. We register the poem's peculiarly doubled character when we ask ourselves: Who claims our interest here, the poetic speaker or the poetic maker, the voice that carries the poem's "transparent upper current of meaning" or the voice that is the "under or *suggestive* one"? (*ER* 337; *CT* 70) Is this a drama of the making of a poem or of the unmaking of a poet?

If we're reading in the same spirit that the author writ, we will be watching both at the same time.[7] Through the making of the poem, the Romantic first person is extinguished as an independent character in the field of the poem. The consequence is a reorientation of the distinction between poetic style and poetic content, the distinction that forms the core of Winters's critique. Winters reads this change as the elimination of content from the poem, a move reflecting, he thinks, Poe's shallow intelligence: he "had a mind for only the crudest of distinctions" (393). But what Poe has actually done is to expose the crudity of Winters's traditional distinction. Winters treats a poem's "style"—its language and versification—as a vehicle for some kind of referent or "content": for a person ("the poet"); a character (the first-person speaker in "The Raven"); an idea, a setting, a narrated or specified action. In Poe's poems, that transactional model of language is refused, just as Poe, in his critique of Charles Babbage's Ninth Bridgewater Treatise, refuses the transactional model of cause and effect as an adequate account of action in the world. What is cause and what is effect depend on the point of view because, as Poe argues, cause and effect are codependent functions.[8]

Poe's poetic moves have large implications for our understanding of the ethics of his poetry. This is very clear from the historical reactions against his aestheticism and art for art's sake. Winters's essay is a signal instance of those reactions. But the ethical questions won't be clearly engaged, I think, until we see exactly how Poe expels a transactional model of language from his poems.

Consider the following passages:

Lo! in yon brilliant window-niche
How statue-like I see thee stand,
The agate lamp within thy hand!
Ah, Psyche, from the regions which
   Are Holy-land! ("To Helen")

How many scenes of what departed bliss!
How many thoughts of what entombéd hopes!
How many visions of a maiden that is
No more— ("Sonnet—To Zante")

Back into the chamber turning, all my soul within me burning,
Soon again I heard a tapping somewhat louder than before.
"Surely," said I, "surely that is something at my window lattice;
Let me see, then, what thereat is, and this mystery explore—
Let my heart be still a moment and this mystery explore;—
  'Tis the wind and nothing more!" ("The Raven")

In all three passages, certain rhymes are so bizarre—niche/which, bliss/that is, and the most startling of all, that is/lattice/thereat is—as to fix our attention on the words and how they sound in our mind's ear, and away from their semantic value. Rhyming a traditional substantive, paradigmatically a noun, with an unrelated pronoun or a syntactic phrase, particularly a phrase whose meaning is quite abstract ("thereat is"), erodes the content value of the one and, reciprocally, assigns substantive force to the abstract action phrase. Or observe in "To Helen" the effect of forcing the weak pronoun "which" to carry both rhyme and strong stress across an enjambment at the poem's climactic moment. Driven into an unnatural prominence, the word suddenly seems unknown and uncanny, as if escaped from "regions which" are regions strange. The move transforms the trivial pronoun to a portentous zeugma and, as such, to an index of the unimaginable "Beauty" that is the poem's subject. And I stress an index rather than a symbol because the poetic event here is strongly performative. The rhyme indicates that a non-normal relation has been made to happen. The consequence is an encounter with a poetical meaning that does not easily yield to an ontological or thematic translation.

Poe's poetry is fairly defined by these kinds of effects, which is why Emerson called him "the jingle man." Like Winters's judgment, Emerson's shows that he has had the experience of Poe's poetry but missed the meaning of the experience. Like Winters, Emerson regards poetry as a vehicle for expressing significant ideas. As such, they require the reader to interpret what they signify. For Poe, on the contrary, poems are compositions of meaningful experience that require from the reader, performance.

Here are some further exemplary moments.

> All Beauty sleeps!—and lo! where lies
> Irenë, with her Destinies! ("The Sleeper")

> So blend the turrets and shadows there
> That all seem pendulous in air,
> While from a proud tower in the town
> Death looks gigantically down.

> But lo, a stir is in the air!
> The wave—there is a movement there! ("The City in the Sea")

> Yes, Heaven is thine; but this
>   Is a world of sweets and sours;
>   Our flowers are merely—flowers,
> And the shadow of thy perfect bliss
>   Is the sunshine of ours. ("Israfel")

What world have we entered in "The Sleeper"? The words "Irenë" and "Destinies" are being worked to suggest more than they could commonly name. In this imaginative landscape, the multiple meanings of Irenë's name call to her multiple sleeping fatalities.[9] Besides, those are Destinies not destinies: quasi-human beings that appear in forms as substantial as the dream that twice comes to Xerxes commanding him to invade Greece.[10]

Or consider those repeated air/there rhymes in "The City in the Sea." The expletive (there) and the adverb (there) are worked to map the landscape being created by the poem itself. In each case, the reader confronts words that, however familiar, suggest that another unknown language lies concealed in our common tongue, as the strange adverb "gigantically" here also shows. When Poe presses the versification to deliver the word to us in five rather than four syllables, that odd form brings special notice to a word whose meaning here is eluding its syntax.

"The Haunted Palace" has a pair of adverbs that get similarly torqued, though in this case they are paired to indicate that an otherworldly music may echo both harmonic and discordant spheres. The word "musically" gets estranged because the verse insists that it be read as four syllables instead of three, and with an odd if clearly called emphasis on the third syllable that comes to preserve the expected rhyme.

> Wanderers in that happy valley,
>> Through two luminous windows, saw
> Spirits moving musically,
>> To a lute's well-tunéd law,   ("The Haunted Palace")

"Musically" here, if strange to our ears, is yet "well-tunéd." Not so the word "fantastically" that comes later in the poem to signal how "evil things" have broken the law of the well-tunéd lute. In this case both syllabification and rhyme are disordered.

And travellers, now, within that valley,
　　Through the encrimsoned windows see
Vast forms that move fantastically
　　To a discordant melody,

While these are unheard melodies in "a world of sweets and sours," in another region—"Out of SPACE, out of TIME"—they are so normal as to resemble the clichés of the unusual lexicon from which Poe draws the language of his poetry.

By a route obscure and lonely,
Haunted by ill angels only,
Where an Eidolon, named NIGHT,
On a black throne reigns upright,
I have reached these lands but newly
From an ultimate dim Thule—
From a wild clime that lieth, sublime,
　　　Out of SPACE—out of TIME.　("Dream-Land")

This clime is beyond even the place named as the ultimate region of the known world, Thule. And the index—again, not the symbol—of such a place is the uncertain pronunciation of the word itself. In our northernmost mortal regions, the Scandinavian world at the edge of Thule, the final vowel of its name is distinctively pronounced short, but as the word descends to the south the vowel grows longer, though it never *truly* rhymes with "newly" even in the British isles. Only in America—Poe's America—does such a rhyme emerge as possible, and when it does, as here, the result is as wonderful and uncanny as the opening couplet of the passage.

The early poem "Al Aaraaf," like Keats's juvenile *Endymion*, is an anthology of the poet's experimental efforts to write this kind of poetry. Poe's *ars poetica* achieves perhaps its most explicit statement, or compositional performance, in Nesace's song to Ligeia in Part II (68–155).

> Where wild flowers, creeping,
>   Have mingled their shade,
> On its margin is sleeping
>   Full many a maid—
> Some have left the cool glade, and
>   Have slept with the bee—
> Arouse them my maiden,
>   On moorland and lea—
> Go! breathe on their slumber,
>   All softly in ear,
> The musical number
>   They slumber'd to hear—   ("Al Aaraaf" II. 136–147)

"The music of [these] things" (II.126) emerges as the unfolding sounds Shade/ maid/ glade, and/ maiden. They signal a poetry of wit, or what Poe called "the fancy."[11] Even more pertinent, it is the wit of a sentimental style, not metaphysical or neoclassical. Its defining character appears as the sequence's ultimate rhyme, which comes, paradoxically, as an invisible but unmistakable presence. It is the unvoiced phrase "made and" that hovers at the end of the passage and, in the context of the song as a whole, specifies, literally, its *poiesis*.[12] Especially remarkable is how this simple rhyme manipulation affects the passage as a whole, implicating other relations, or what Poe calls "equalities" in "The Rationale of Verse." The unvoiced "made and" works through the initial rhyme of "glade" and "maid." "Glade" comes to the "aid" of "maid." The rhyme thus gets "mingled" as well with an all-but-explicit synesthesia: the shade cast by the flowers conceals the fragrance that becomes the breath of Ligeia, which transforms to the sound heard by the sleeping maidens.

II

In writing this way, Poe was studying Shelley and Tennyson. But he invented other, analogous devices for releasing his poetry to what he called "The Power of Words." Some of the most striking moments in "Israfel" emerge when he punctuates its fantastical discourse with words from a decidedly low, even comic, lexicon.

In Heaven a spirit doth dwell
   "Whose heart-strings are a lute;"
None sing so wildly well
As the angel Israfel,
And the giddy stars (so legends tell)
Ceasing their hymns, attend the spell
   Of his voice, all mute.

Tottering above
   In her highest noon,
   The enamoured moon
Blushes with love,

"Giddy," "tottering," "blushes": the poetry is struck from "unusual strings" (22), a phrase that itself "totters," like the giddy stars, at the edge of poetical decorum. At each of the poem's moves toward Israfel's transmortal "Heaven," it gets braked from soaring. Sometimes the brake is applied by an art of words that sink away from "The ecstasies above" ("Merrily live, and long"; "sweets and sours"). But Poe's unusual strings play with correspondent syntaxes, as we see in the elliptical form of lines 37–38:

> The ecstacies above
>   With thy burning measures suit—
> Thy grief, thy joy, thy hate, thy love,
>   With the fervour of thy lute—
> Well may the stars be mute! (35–39)

Even more striking is the interrupted syntax in the previous two stanzas:

> But the skies that angel trod,
>   Where deep thoughts are a duty—
> Where Love's a grown-up God—
>   Where the Houri glances are
> Imbued with all the beauty
>   Which we worship in a star.
>
> Therefore, thou art not wrong,
>   Israfeli, who despisest
> An unimpassioned song (23–31)

"Therefore"? The word is doubly mysterious, partly because we can't see how it follows from the previous stanza. And that puzzle gets further complicated because the thought of the previous stanza, after careful syntactic elaboration, is left unfinished.

Most arresting of all is the dazzling wordplay of "Israfel's" second stanza:

Tottering above
   In her highest noon,
   The enamoured moon
Blushes with love,
   While, to listen, the red levin
   (With the rapid Pleiads, even,
   Which were seven,)
   Pauses in Heaven. (8–15)

The lines start by troping on a recognizable astronomic event: the emergence of a reddening moon as it plunges into full lunar eclipse, which the poem later recalls as "the shadow of [Israfel's] perfect bliss" (43). Like the arrested lightning, the moon's color is a sublunar reflection of "Israfeli's fire" (18), which burns purely—unaffected by our mortal atmosphere—somewhere even beyond the distant fires of the Pleiads. The initial tight image of a love-drunken moon is spilling into a set of enskied images that are at once irrational, slightly ambiguous, and yet sharply defined. The complexities seem particularly rich, first of all because they are not based on contradictions but on unexpected junctures created from shifting conceptual points of view that are acoustically defined. Even more important, the images strain against a pair of controlling formalities: the repeated end rhymes and, most of all, the involuted, pedantic syntax. The stanza is a wonder of unblemished "Affectation."

This kind of poetic complex resembles nothing so much as one of Emily Dickinson's "impacted poems," except that in Poe's case we don't have to fight through a savagely elliptical syntax.[13] As

Poe's stanza flaunts its intention to literal clarity—once again, the language is not symbolistic—word references are set adrift, and we seem to glimpse unknown realities operating within the natural and quotidian order of things.

The effect is achieved paradoxically because the poem covets such declarative precision, as in the opening stanza. After quoting George Sale's "Preliminary Discourse" to his influential scholarly translation of the Koran,[14] the lines invoke more ancient authorities who have explained the effect of "the spell/ Of [Israfel's] voice" on other angelic singers. Although the record of such "legends" is unpreserved by Sale or any other scholar, the poetic syntax uniquely declares their truth, first by parenthetical aside, and finally by a significant afterthought. The syntax is as cunning as it is careful, however, for "all mute" is a double appositive referencing two figures of transmortal silence.

So the method of Poe's poetry is less a function of what it means than of how it works. We have to parse with great care its procedural complexities, and in particular the regular play between its music-based versification and its prose syntax. Equally important is Poe's lexicon, which here, as so often, is drawn from the discourse of sentimental cliché and the popular culture of his period. A poem like "Eldorado," for example, shows how much can be made by pressing a single rhyme on the poem's title and then running that rhyme through a series of attendant rhymes. The complex rhyming cluster keeps returning the reader to the poem's keyword, each time slightly shifting our angle of attention. This move argues (procedurally) that the word *is* what it appears to be, but that its appearances need careful attention. For a double historical meaning shadows the title word. One is quasi-legendary, the other is contemporary, and both are deeply American. Putting the reader to a test of those two meanings, the poem evolves a third meaning as a poetical "under current."

The clichés of the opening couplet immediately reference the early plundering expeditions into the New World and the Conquistador legend of a lost city of gold that grew out of those marauding adventures. All of that is slightly but certainly ironized by the obsolete language, and the illusion of the quest is plainly determined by the end of the second stanza. Running through those historical recollections is a parallel contemporary event (the poem was published in the spring of 1849): the California Gold Rush (1848–1853), which the popular press was everywhere calling the new search for Eldorado.[15] We don't have to recall Poe's personal contempt for the Gold Rush craze to recognize the critical position the poem is taking toward a pair of his favorite subjects: self-delusion and crass American materialism.[16]

Even as those critical views have unfolded, however, the poem suddenly pivots at the beginning of stanza three, when the adventurer's "strength/ Failed him at length."[17] At that point he meets his spiritual double "the pilgrim shadow" and asks him "Where" to find Eldorado. The shadow answers:

"Over the Mountains
        Of the Moon,
Down the Valley of the Shadow,
        Ride, boldly ride,"
        The shade replied,—
"If you seek for Eldorado!"

Note that the pilgrim does not tell where to seek but how to seek. The reply implicitly argues the error in imagining Eldorado as an actual place. Eldorado is not a place but either a psychological state (personal) or a social condition (ideology) or, as here, both. The poem thus emerges as a test of the reader that echoes the sibylline words of the pilgrim shadow to the American adventurer. Passing each test entails being clear about what the word *Eldorado* means and how the poem "Eldorado" works.

But there is more, for if the pilgrim casts a cold eye on both the Conquistadors and the Gold Rush craze, his words positively endorse even more fantastic adventures. Negotiating the intellectual hazard of this little poem reveals the "under current" of meaning in the word and legend of Eldorado. Seen properly (according to Poe), Eldorado names "the desire of the moth for the star." Seen properly, it will therefore also always be seen "through a glass, darkly," as the final stanza emphasizes. But for Poe, that fatality is far less chastening—though it *is* that—than it is at once ominous and inspiriting: "Ride, boldly ride." That would be Poe's version of Blake's Proverb of Hell: "If the fool would persist in his folly he would become wise."

So much of Poe's poetry depends upon exposing the unremarked significance of otherwise unremarkable things. Acutely entertained, even the most dessicated language—"Gaily bedight," for instance—possesses an undying vital instinct. The unheard melodies of Poe's uncanny world are thus closely tied to a poetry of popular commonplace, conventional scenes, characters and events, and clichéd linguistic forms. So we register the transhuman character of Israfel's music because it is linked to such a quotidian word, "unusual." An unusual word to apply to such a fabulous creature, Poe chooses it to sound a mortal echo of Israfel's immortal music.

Poe's poetry becomes an acoustical dictionary of phrase and fable where complex relations of assonance and consonance—"combinations of combinations"—shift the language until it tilts at the edge of normality. The effect starts from simple phrases—"agate lamp," "wilderness of glass," "sulphurous currents down Yaanek"—and multiplies through longer sequences.

> Up many and many a marvellous shrine
> Whose wreathed friezes intertwine
> The viol, the violet, and the vine. ("The City in the Sea")

> By a route obscure and lonely,
> Haunted by ill angels only, ("Dream-Land")

> Then, methought, the air grew denser, perfumed from an unseen
>   censer
> Swung by Seraphim whose foot-falls tinkled on the tufted floor.
> ("The Raven")

> Astarte's bediamonded crescent,
> Distinct with its duplicate horn. ("Ulalume")

While imagery and literary allusion have their parts to play in those passages, the predominant power is acoustic. And if we fill out the context of that last example we see how quickly the normal world can be undone by a resolute application of simple repetition with variation:

> And now, as the night was senescent,
>   And star-dials pointed to morn—
>   As the star-dials hinted of morn—
> At the end of our path a liquescent
>   And nebulous lustre was born,

Out of which a miraculous crescent
  Arose with a duplicate horn—
Astarte's bediamonded crescent,
  Distinct with its duplicate horn. ("Ulalume" 30–38)

An impressive body of scholarship attends upon this poetry because its language is at once so particular and so elusive. Readers work hard to specify references that might stand behind (and then help to explain) the poetry, as if careful annotation would give a means for controlling the work's catastrophic energies. While such scholarship is indispensable, it can be quite misleading if it suggests that the poetry requires the external control of translation or decoding. The following lines illustrate both the virtue of such scholarship and the danger it represents for the poetry.

It was hard by the dim lake of Auber,
  In the misty mid region of Weir:—
It was down by the dank tarn of Auber,
  In the ghoul-haunted woodland of Weir. ("Ulalume" 6–9)

Mabbott, the most learned of all Poe scholars, has two extensive notes on the strange words "Auber" and "Weir." It turns out that Poe neither invented those words nor lifted them from an atlas or gazetteer. They are the names of two contemporaries whose work he would have known about: the theatrical composer Daniel-François-Esprit Auber (1782–1871) and the Hudson River School painter Robert Walter Weir (1803–1889). Knowing those names is useful exactly because they do *not* establish the meaning of the words they become in the poem. The *words* establish the meaning as they are simply words, not as they are *names,* for Poe has transubstantiated those personal names by treating them as phonetic things. Here they have turned into names for a place as unimagined as the "It" by which the narrator repeatedly specifies and locates that place.[18]

No poem better exhibits that way with language than "The Raven," Poe's forecast of Stevens's Snowman, unfolding "nothing that is not there and the nothing that is." Flaunting its artifactuality, the poem keeps calling our attention to itself as an unfolding textual event:

> Back into the chamber turning, all my soul within me burning,
> Soon again I heard a tapping somewhat louder than before.
> "Surely," said I, "surely that is something at my window lattice;
> Let me see, then, what thereat is, and this mystery explore—
> Let my heart be still a moment and this mystery explore." (31–35)

"That is"/"lattice"/"thereat is": these are Poe's textual tappings provoking us to explore the apparent mysteries of the poem. But the mysteries are not hidden away; they are all in perfect view if we would simply pay attention, for instance, to the mysterious and amusing charm of those arbitrary multiple rhymings. One recalls not only "The Purloined Letter" but Poe's comment in his early theoretical "Letter to B——": "As regards the greater truths, men oftener err by seeking them at the bottom than at the top; . . . in the palpable" (CT 7).

Artifice, the mystery of human creativity, is therefore to be exposed, not confused with surplus mysteriousness and its unhelpful unapparencies. All that Poe derides as "Transcendentalism." Perhaps no passage in the poem makes a more startling display of his view than the following:

> Then this ebony bird beguiling my sad fancy into smiling,
> By the grave and stern decorum of the countenance it wore,

> "Though thy crest be shorn and shaven, thou," I said, "art sure no
>   craven,
> Ghastly grim and ancient Raven wandering from the Nightly
>   shore—
> Tell me what thy lordly name is on the Night's Plutonian shore!"
>   Quoth the Raven, "Nevermore." (43–48)

The passage throws in our face—by way of our ears, if I may so put the matter—certain dazzling verbal transformations. As we know from contemporary rhyming dictionaries plus the example of many poets, decorum held that the *g* terminating an *-ing* ending is an unvoiced letter in poetry. This rule brings Shelley, for example, to the following rhyme: "And we shrank back—for dreams of ruin / To frozen caves our flight pursuing" (*Prometheus Unbound* I.103–104). Knowing this rule, as Poe's readers did, they were being beguiled into smiling at the double transformation flirting in the phrase "Raven wandering." For that would be (also) to say "Raven wanderin.'" But juxtaposing precisely *those* two words licenses further transformational actions. Words terminating in a short *e* or *i* followed by an *n* become seeable as having undergone a literal, orthographic elision, so that the phrase also transforms to mean "raving wandering." The transformations metastasize, affecting nearby texts (*craven* transforms nicely into *craving*). In fact, the whole system of the poem is undergoing a transformational invasion. Did we think we understood the title of Poe's poem? Did we know when we first read it that it also meant "The Raving"?

Or most beguiling of all such transformations, when do we realize that *raven* is virtually *never* spelled backwards?[19]

Crucially, while all of those verbal effects come to us through a first-person—indeed, as the text implies, a poet—he appears estranged from his own words. The text thus unfolds as an independent action, the poetic composition becoming an explanation of his virtually willful and self-absorbed "loneliness unbroken" (100). Read as a psychological study, it presents a person traumatized in loss: at first cherishing a blithe unawareness of his pain until it gradually imposes itself and forces a direct confrontation. At that point he recoils altogether, embracing what Byron called "The cherished madness of my heart" (*The Giaour* 1191). The final two stanzas carry Poe's narrator to his dreadful commitment to conscious darkness.

But, as "The Philosophy of Composition" argues, the poem is only incidentally a study of psychic derangement. The poetic composition turns that psychological drama to an index of the kind of poetry being deplored in the essay. Like the essay, the poem is telling the story of two kinds of poets and two kinds of poetry. In one, the figure of the poet appears lost and consumed by his own affective life. In the other, that scene of personal experience—in a word, the poet's "sincerity"—is irrelevant to the poetic action. The figure of the Romantic poet disappears as the verbal action of the poem—which includes the poetic narrative—is objectively reconceived. If we are aware of "the poet" at all, he appears, like an absent God, only in and as the real presence of the work itself. This is the Poe that Whitman, like the many others who have praised his "brilliance," celebrate: Poe as virtuoso and technician.

Pertinent as that Poe must be, he is an entirely secondary Poe, just as a care for verse technique—Poe's "inferior and less capable music"—is secondary to the principal work of poetry.[20] As he makes clear, verse and poetry are as distinct from each other as "the *physique* [from] the *morale* of music," or technique from imagination. But because "metre, rhythm, and rhyme" have such deep and extensive historical relations—are "of so vast a *moment* in Poetry" (my italics)—they are "never to be wisely rejected" or dispensed with. They are useful for multiplying "equalities"—"combinations, and combinations of combinations"—and realizing the presence of "bodily thought." More important still, they estrange the poetry from the poet, hurling the texts (impossibly) toward that Absolute condition that Mallarmé was among the first to perceive was the clear object, and subject, of Poe's poetry. The speaker in "The Raven" and the poet of "The Raven" are both alienated and as such are signature Poetic doubles: the speaker's psychic and mortal derangement reflecting the poet's willful estrangement, demonic and—if we take the word as Shelley and Swinburne used it—divine.

III

"The Raven" has what Stevens called "a mind of winter"—more exactly, two minds of winter. As the speaker's mind journeys to its final stasis in the pallid land of affectless "shadow," the poet's has grown incorporate with the journeying text, indifferent, machinic, impersonal. Only the reader remains a human presence to the poem, which has been forcing us to confront its dark representations. The speaker's final passivity is certainly horrible, but more trying still is the poem's cold address in face of both of its subjects: the tale it tells and the audience to whom it delivers that tale.

A few years later (1852) Matthew Arnold would publish a poem, *Empedocles on Etna,* that put its reader in a like situation. Reading it again shortly after it appeared, Arnold's moral sense recoiled from what he had done:

What then are the situations, from the representation of which, though accurate, no poetical enjoyment can be derived? They are those in which the suffering finds no vent in action; in which a continuous state of mental distress is prolonged, unrelieved by incident, hope, or resistance; in which there is everything to be endured, nothing to be done. In such situations there is inevitably something morbid, in the description of them something monotonous. When they occur in actual life, they are painful, not tragic; the representation of them in poetry is painful also.

To this class of situations, poetically faulty as it appears to me, that of Empedocles, as I have endeavored to represent him, belongs; and I have therefore excluded the poem from the present collection. "Preface," *Poems* (1853)

Arnold's account perfectly reflects the trial of the reader that Poe made the central purpose of his work. "The Raven" leaves its readers with everything to be endured and nothing to be done. The poem is doubly inexorable: it winds out its tale of a catatonic condition and does nothing to mitigate, much less to resist and least of all to cure or purge, the affective hell into which we are drawn. In an important sense—Whitman once again is the best witness here—what is most unendurable is the poem's "demoniac undertone," as if (like the demoniac poet and poem) we were expected to be "enjoying all the terror, the murk, and the dislocation." The comical moments that punctuate the first half of the poem, and that the speaker himself initially indulges, dramatize this new kind of "poetical enjoyment" Poe is cultivating.

"The Conqueror Worm" works up a literally spectacular representation of Poe's new Poetics. It is opening night of a new production of the ancient and familiar tragedy *Man,* with a packed audience of angels come to watch a "play of hopes and fears" that are, in fact, the hopes and fears the "lunary" angels share with sublunary Man. But the poem has invited its mortal audience— ourselves—to watch that play in a larger theatrical setting: the play called *The Conqueror Worm* in which *Man* is a theatrical in- terlude, or a play within a play. Stage, backstage, orchestra, and auditorium provide the setting for this enveloping play's virtually cosmic action. Cosmic *and* comic, however, for the perspective of the poem miniaturizes everything it represents: the sentimental angels ("drowned in tears"), an incompetent orchestra blunder- ing through "the music of the spheres," and inarticulate puppet- like actors who appear "in the form of God on high" because— this is Poe's perverse joke—they are made, as we know, in His image and likeness. The second stanza is an especially effective piece of grotesque humor:

Mimes, in the form of God on high,
    Mutter and mumble low,
And hither and thither fly—
    Mere puppets they, who come and go
At bidding of vast formless things
    That shift the scenery to and fro,
Flapping from out their Condor wings
    Invisible Woe! (9–16)

This is a fantastical restaging of the clumsy spectacles mounted in the American theatres where Poe's parents performed and where he was a regular critic. The textual scene hangs on the self-consciously gothic phrase "Condor wings," a clear recollection of the tableau

137

curtains that were common at the time, particularly in smaller theatres with severely restricted backstage and wing spaces. The curtains are drawn up and back so that they appear to hover at the stage wings, whence they can be quickly dropped ("comes down with the rush of a storm") to cover noisy scenery changes. The poem mocks the frantic and ineffectual stage illusions attempted by the various theater agents: not only the "mimic rout" of puppet-actors but, even more grotesquely, the "vast formless things" operating offstage, "invisible" agents setting in motion woes that are now, through Poe's risible restaging, doubly invisible, unseen and unreal.

Comical as this must appear to anyone observing it from "on high," its exposed irreality—Poe's comic irony—only reinforces the fearful power of illusionist affect. The transmortal angels are horror-struck (stage struck) at the spectacle of the mortal lifeworld, which for them is the unimaginable unknown, a truly Fearful revelation even as it is also and manifestly Absurd (a "blood-red thing that writhes from out/ The scenic solitude"). After all, angels aren't the only ones known to be afraid of death. Stanza three marks the poem's vision of Madness, Sin, and Horror as the motley and phantasmatic consequences of a transcendental consciousness. At the same time, the stanza lets us know that this play has had a long run and "shall not be forgot." For it tells the tale of a "Phantom chased for evermore/ By a crowd that seize it not." Of course, that would be "sees" as well as "seize."

Or rather and more darkly (now that Poe has remounted the ancient tragedy): by a crowd that seeing, they do not see, and hearing, they do not understand. An audience-enlightenment follows from the anagnorisis in classical tragedy, purging the access of pity and fear raised by the action. No such result comes with the action of Poe's poem. Indeed, the fact that enlightenment pervades the poem from the start—that the poem is poised in self-awareness—defines the metatragical (or seriocomical) character of Poe's vision. And so the poem builds toward a new kind of discovery or "under current" of thought: that enlightenment itself, not least aesthetic enlightenment, is the "food" on which human Fear and Illusion feed and thrive. In Manfred's famous declaration: "The Tree of Knowledge is not that of Life" (*Manfred* I. 1. 12).

So at the end of Poe's new theatrical production, the Condor curtain drops "with the rush of a storm," and the house lights go not up but entirely out. The scene resembles nothing so much as Benjamin reading Klee's *Angel of History* as an emblem of the dreadful storms of the paradisal and angelic imagination.[21] Like Benjamin, history has swept Poe away into the "mournful and never ending remembrance" of "what shall not be forgot": the endlessly repeating story of human loss. Immortal birds are not born for death, it is true, but mortal ones—poets who are also persons, like Keats and Poe—definitely are. So for Poe, there is nothing tender in that enveloping night. At the same time, as Whitman saw, the Poetic darkness and storm is neither fled from nor resented in this poem. At the same time, as we can see, no escape from the tumult is either imagined or hoped for. The poem is entirely "centre and victim."

Poe discussed the poem's general framework of thought in the letter he wrote to Lowell in July 1844, where he has a "reverie of the future" that is grounded in the past imperfect. He does not ask us to read his poetic drama from "the point of view of Eternity"—"of God on high"—but from the point of view of the Mimes of Memory, of which this poem is one. The redemption of the present for Poe is only imaginable in the salvation of "the foregone time" and the "individual[s]" whom we must count "on an equal footing with ourselves." But because whole hosts of those individuals stand forever outside the economy of Christian grace, on one hand, and real mortal presence, on the other, "salvation" for Poe means casting the perpetual and imperfect light of memory upon the dead. Like the letter to Lowell, Poe's poem mounts a critical reflection on the ideology of "progress" and "perfectibility," the nineteenth-century's secular translation of Christian redemption. A Human Comedy of cherished loss comes to underpin a Divine Comedy of future promise—more precisely, comes to argue that cherished loss is the love that birthed the Divine Comedy in the first place.[22] For "Man is in love and loves what vanishes" ("Nineteen Hundred Nineteen").

The poem that deals most acutely with Poe's remarkable aesthetics of Memory is "Ulalume." It is a modern ballad story about how it means (rather than what it means) to live in a Time out of Mind, which for Poe might well define the human condition *per se*. From the first to the last stanza—to *both* last stanzas— "Ulalume" compels us to experience that condition.[23] The poem thus implicitly argues that the condition, rather like Time itself, is conceptually inaccessible. But the condition is neither experientially nor linguistically inaccessible. Poetic mimesis can build a simulation machine for readers.

The basic narrative—but not the basic narration—is simple: the speaker tells how he took a journey that ends when he discovers he had already taken exactly the same journey. The story gets immensely complicated, however, because the poem develops a framework of elaborate temporal uncertainties. The effect is to move our experience of the poem "through a circle that ever returneth in/ To the self-same spot" ("The Conqueror Worm," 20–21). The first stanza is severely recollective ("It was") but tilts slightly when the second stanza, also past tense, opens with the word "Here," a move that is reinforced at the beginning of stanza four ("And now"). That complication is again complicated toward the close of the third stanza when the speaker remarks parenthetically that "once" before they had made this journey, though neither he nor his soul remembered (note the past tense!) doing so. The vertiginous prospect that we glimpse in this strange unremembered memory is quickly shut down when we move into the "now" of the fourth stanza and the sudden appearance of Astarte. While the remainder of the poem is a report of past events—what "past" would that be, we increasingly wonder?—our experience of the report is dominated by a present-tense conversational exchange between the speaker and his soul, Psyche.

The effect of an arrested time/stalled temporality—of a past and a present that are both always only "here" and "now"—is established in the first stanza:

The skies they were ashen and sober;
    The leaves they were crispéd and sere—
    The leaves they were withering and sere:
It was night, in the lonesome October
    Of my most immemorial year:
It was hard by the dim lake of Auber,
    In the misty mid region of Weir:—
It was down by the dank tarn of Auber,
    In the ghoul-haunted woodland of Weir.

The stanza keeps forcing the temporal markers "they were" and "It was" into particular things located in a specific condition that is dominantly spatial rather than temporal. Shifting the pronominal phrases "they were" to the repeated expletive phrases ("It was night," "It was hard by," "It was down by") completes the transformation of an event—something has happened though we don't know what it is—into a scene. The effect unhinges the word "October" from the solar calendar and assigns it a function in the temporality of the "star dials" (31), the horologue of the transtemporal order which is unfolding in Poe's poem.

The imaginative action of the stanza centers in the notorious phrase "my most immemorial year." Far from being an example of linguistic imprecision, as Eliot thought, it demonstrates why, under certain conditions of expressive emergency, only perfect nonsense—perfect contradiction—will serve. The phrase names a year that is a function of multiple contradictory conditions: it is a year in the life of this particular speaker, but a year that is not only very old (as in Tennyson's "immemorial elms"), it is more than that: it is entirely beyond even the oldest temporal order (as in the phrase "time immemorial").[24] Poe's novel (mis)usage—a staple move in nonsense verse and riddle poetry—manages to make this both a year in the life of the speaker and a year beyond either his or anyone else's life. Adding the superlative "most"—superlatively supererogatory—perfects the realization of an impossible time. (The perhaps equally notorious line in "Annabel Lee," "We loved with a love that was more than love," is clearly fashioned out of the same kind of imaginative effort.)

The poem's uncanny effects receive a decisive formulation in stanza three. As the conventional ballad repetition echoes stanza one—and underscores the dramatic artifactuality of the poem—it also calls attention to the speaker, who has been positioned in the poem exactly as the angels were positioned in "The Conqueror

Worm" or this speaker's counterpart in "The Raven." In each case, the reader has a parallel but more comprehensive view of the unfolding events. While we are reading "Ulalume," its speaker is still caught up in the poetic narrative he is himself delivering. We hear the echoes of stanza one, but the speaker, though he utters the echoing words, is unaware of the memory they represent. But our reader's knowledge is at this point still incomplete. Not until the speaker and Psyche together finally confront the tomb (stanza eight, ll. 72–81) do we realize the truth of his condition: that he cannot remember what he cannot forget. Psyche's "mistrust" (52) as well as his own confidence (61–71) together signal—did we miss this when we were reading?—that the speaker's amnesia measures the depth of his immemorial sorrow.

That sorrow is especially dreadful because it is less a psychic condition than a poetical figure of deep estrangement that is available to the reader and not the speaker. It cannot be too emphatically stressed that the speakers in Poe's poems are poetic devices and not the poems' subject of attention. The reader is Poe's subject. That is why his poetry builds an environment of Fear that suffuses the poems and that is the hallmark of his writing. Poetic Fear does not come to us primarily as the psychic state of a central character like the speaker of "Ulalume" but as an objectified condition intended to affect the reader. This poem brings that condition to its disturbingly clear crisis in the tenth stanza when the poem's dialogue of Self and Soul collapses. But instead of marking Self and Soul as "we two then" speaking together, as we might say "with one voice," the poem performs its definitive act of cold estrangement when it writes, as it were on its own, "the two then."

The implication throughout—that a mysterious fate controls the second journey—gets foregrounded in stanzas 4–7 (ll. 30–71), a thoroughly fantastical description of the rising of the planet Venus at early predawn. The poem recasts this otherwise common natural event into a form weighted with astrological and premonitory import. Of greatest significance is the general recollection of Byron's *Manfred*. Setting the figure of Astarte above this central section of the poem's action inevitably maps the speaker's quest for "Lethean peace" (45) to Manfred's world-famous quest for "Forgetfulness" and "Oblivion—self-oblivion" (*Manfred* I. 1. 91, 144). In Byron's play, Manfred's beloved, Astarte, rises out of darkness like the rising planet in "Ulalume"—from a "limbo of lunary souls" (102) even. As here in "Ulalume," Astarte's appearance drives Manfred back to a memory that he desperately wants to forget. In the end, Manfred joins Astarte in death and utters the famous last words that would echo across the entire nineteenth century to their late reception in Nietzsche: "'tis not so difficult to die" (*Manfred* III. 4. 151). Like the unrevealed "secret that lies hid in [the] wolds" (98) of "Ulalume," Manfred never explains the exact cause of his initial desperation, though we know he judges himself guilty of the death of Astarte.

But at the end of *Manfred,* however mysterious its situation, we have no doubt that Manfred has found psychic peace. The poem shows us the final perplexity of the monk and Manfred's retainers in order to underscore the magnitude of Manfred's triumph. The end of "Ulalume" is very different, whether we read it with or without stanza 10. Without those lines, we are left with the image of the Self and the Soul fixed in a condition of conscious trauma. With stanza 10, the scene is even more ominous and unresolved, as the stanza's series of thoroughly ambiguous questions show. The "dread burden" (87) the speaker brought on his first journey—by gothic implication, the corpse of Ulalume—has grown far heavier, more woeful. However a reader struggles with the final unanswerable questions, there is no doubt that Poe's ghouls have robbed the grave of Byron in order to bring Ulalume back as well, lest her irrevocable loss be forgotten.

4

The Politics of a Poetry
without Politics

୫ଠ

Yes, forsooth: I wish you joy o' the worm.

Shakespeare, *Antony and Cleopatra*
V. ii. 278

I

Although Poe's career spanned a seriously fractious and volatile period, he rarely comments on the social and political events of his time. His difference in this respect from Bryant, Cooper, Lowell, Longfellow, and the Transcendentalist Circle is striking. Poe's public interests are intense, but they are also narrowly circumscribed, and media-directed, as his long passion to found a distinguished literary and cultural journal shows. When he does comment, however, he doesn't mince words, nor does he set himself apart from judgment.

> We, of the nineteenth century, need some worker of miracles for our regeneration; but so degraded have we become that the only prophet, or preacher, who could render us much service, would be the St. Francis who converted the beasts.
>
> (*Marginalia* June 1849, M 193)

146

Because he rarely descends to detail or even general comment on contemporary events, the political importance of Poe's work is easy to mistake. For all his admiration of Shelley, he is not that kind of missioned spirit. He is skeptical, often contemptuous, of enlightened social views. Yet he had a far deeper understanding of the vulgarity, hypocrisy, and violence of antebellum America than Frances Trollope or the other European visitors who so annoyed Americans with their critical reports. He had an insider's view. But he was more than an alien resident, he was an alienated player, as active and even unscrupulous in advancing his special interests as anyone. That complex antithetical position has often been held against him, and against his poetry in particular, especially by the authorities of High Culture. Even when a reader tries to meet him on even footing, as J. T. Barbarese recently did in an otherwise very attractive essay, the terms are unequal. For Barbarese, "The Sleeper," which Poe regarded as his greatest poem, is simply "hack" work—a mishmash of romantic clichés and figural common-places.[1] Like so many, Barbarese has a quarrel with Poe's tools.

As with Schopenhauer, Poe's is a world of Will and Representation. It is, like Schopenhauer's, a world of darkness because it is mapped to the illusions that organized his world, its foundational ideologies. That focus, Poe's special map, has serious critical virtues. Two in particular are notable because they are so characteristic of his work.

First, the discourse of popular culture defines Poe's poetic discourse, which often draws upon the grammars and dictionaries of sensibility in their most recent Romantic editions—very much trade editions. Like his cultural contemporaries, popular as well as critical, Poe is an assiduous student of English Romanticism as it rises in Wordsworth and Coleridge and peaks in Shelley,

Moore, Keats, and Byron, and finally in Tennyson's Romantic doom.[2]

His poetry is often deplored as impossibly abstract and derivative—a spilled and threadbare Romanticism. The charge is understandable, even correct in a way, but finally misconceived— or perhaps I should say that it refuses to read in the same spirit that the author writ. It issues from a vantage like that of Yvor Winters, who expects poetic language to have a strong referential content, cognitive or concrete. But Winters's rationale for that expectation, which rightly draws upon the deliberately memorial character of poetry, has forgotten how memory works in poetic mimesis. Poetry holds a mirror up to the world—the poet's particular world—in the language of that world, which includes the languages it inherits and retransmits. To say, in a remote idiom, that memory is the mother of the muses is exactly the same as saying, in a more contemporary idiom, that it is a consciously intertextual discourse. Poe's poetry is unusual because it marks itself as such: a mournful and never-ending remembrance, haunted in intertext.

His discourse is thus grounded in self-conscious forms of representation. It is a mediated, ideological discourse. These forms are very precise as forms, but like the language of dreams, the forms are encoded. From our point of view, the most important thing about these coded discursions is that they are left uninterpreted at the level of the poetic expression—a provocative condition that has led not a few readers to seek interpretive resolutions for Poe's "poetics of opacity."[3] To provide explanatory devices would be, for Poe, Didactic Heresy. And as he knew, didacticism can take many forms, the least insidious being direct moral or political comment. For Poe, the most insidious is conventional narrative and its rules of probability.

Poe's poetry has to be read the way we read Rimbaud's, especially the *Illuminations*. In English, Hart Crane's poetry provides a close analogue, as Yvor Winters himself suggested when he applied the same word to Crane's poetry—"catastrophe"—as to Poe's.[4] Even more interesting is the example of Emily Dickinson, and especially the group of disturbingly "impacted poems" that David Porter found most characteristic of her "Modern Idiom."[5] Those works set a standard for the difficulties that Dickinson's poetry has never ceased to raise. Obscurities and uncanny effects are staple in all of these writers, as we know, but what makes their work so distinctive is its conscious, even flaunted, artifice. Poe, Dickinson, Rimbaud, and Crane mark their obscurities as deliberated fabrications. As such, readers are put on notice that Shelley's "veil of familiarity" of known poetic conventions is being consciously stripped bare in order to reveal "the naked and sleeping beauty, which is the spirit of its forms" ("A Defence of Poetry," *Shelley's Poetry and Prose*, 505). The result, in Hart Crane's words, is poetry poised at "new thresholds" and formed of "new anatomies" ("The Wine Menagerie," 29).[6] It calls for an interpretive response that is equal to the self-conscious work that so challenges our attention. When traditional meanings and referential forms are drawn into this poetry, as they always (and necessarily) are, they become subject to a transvaluation of their customary values. As we've already seen, the engine driving those transvaluations in Poe is a musical composition of hitherto unheard melodies

To see the poetry as intertextual means seeing it as a medium of the political unconscious. Poems, as Tennyson might say, moan round with many voices that are then reassembled in a new poetical present. The intertextuality of Poe's poetry is so unusually naked and insistent, however, that readers are drawn to pay attention not to what the texts mean but to how those voices—*nos semblables, nos frères*—continue to make meanings for us and we for them. We've discussed this already as the style of Poe's musical formalities because such an understanding of Poe is fundamental. Because the intertexts have social and historical dimensions, readers are also summoned to notice how these dimensions inflect the poetic meanings. Readers are the ones who finally make poetic meanings, and, of course, the poets are their own first readers. That priority of reading signals why we later readers must begin to read in the same spirit that the author writ before we go on to read in any kind of counter-spirit. "How are you reading the work of these summoned spirits?" is ultimately the question that the poems are putting to us. The procedure is strongly reminiscent of the challenging effect of Ahab's doubloon.

All semiotic forms translate eventual experience into conceptual terms that allow us to reflect and communicate. Imaginative writing—poetry in particular—recovers an experiential engagement with those conceptual translations. Language, rhetoric, bibliography, and media display are always specific to time and place and circumstance, and an alert critical philology can and should expose those specifics and their intertextual connections. In the case of Poe's poetry, the absence of manifest referential content, its aggressively literary and formal qualities, have led many readers to search the poetry for a reliable biographical ground, or to seek out coded references to race, politics, and gender. But in reading Poe we have to be specially wary of all such moves since they can so easily lead us to retranslate the work back into conceptual—Poe called them "Didactic"—terms. Poe's great subject is poetic representation itself, and the deeper truth is that he takes this to be an imperative social and political subject.

Poe's poetic method thus carries a second and even more consequential virtue, though in another, perhaps deeper sense, this
virtue is, like Ahab's doubloon, seriously problematic. His discourse holds a mirror up to his contemporary world's hall of mirrors and its will to romantic representations.

Consider his notorious misogyny. Unlike Baudelaire's dandiacal
revulsion, Poe's attitude to women fed upon widespread nineteenth-
century sentimental ideas. Like nearly all of his contemporaries,
including many of the period's most prominent women, he cherished an idealized feminine figure—both as *ewig weibliche* and as
belle idéale. His attitude, a legacy of the eighteenth-century Sentimental Enlightenment, mirrors his serious interest in and promo-
tion of contemporary women's poetry. The term for this figure,
characteristically antebellum, was True Woman.[7]

Odd as it might seem, this feminine (not feminist) mystique
has much in common with the thinking of reformers like Mary
Wollstonecraft and Margaret Fuller. On the other hand, no such
congruities appear if we compare Poe's views with the Grimkes'
open and far less compromised campaign to promote women's
social and political responsibilities under the rubric of The New
Woman.[8] Poe had no interest in seeing women enter the public
sphere or in promoting women's civic rights. He adhered to the
view, dominant at the time, that women's public function was to
reign supreme in the private sphere. But Poe's other and chief
interest—in the discourse of poetry and imagination—turned his
retrograde social view into a critical weapon.

Helen (or "Helen") was the towering soul presiding in those
"regions which/ Are holy land"—a mythic counter-world and
counterculture bringing judgment to the world Emerson declared
full "of perjury and fraud in a hundred commodities."[9] Poe's (in)

famous instrument of judgment is the imaginative device he drew out of the Dantescan myth recovered by the Romantics: "The death of a beautiful woman." This is Poe's "most poetical subject in the world" in two respects. First of all, the figure organizes Poe's imaginative world as an ideological condition, a literary and cultural inheritance, an intertext. Secondly, the figure is a gravity field for the cultural condition of the nineteenth-century, the epoch of High Romanticism and its immediate aftermath.[10] "The Raven" is not just signature Poe, it is also period-signature, as its fame and scandal alike testify. Bird poems are everywhere from Wordsworth to Hardy, and so are figurations of dead and dying women.

So simplified has our thought become about Poe's notorious remark, and so attenuated our memory, that we would do well to reflect on the astonishing array of dead and beautiful women scattered across the field of the nineteenth century. Even the sentimental figures are scarcely one-dimensional victims, as a quick review of their company will show: Wordsworth's Lucy is nothing like Cooper's Narrah-mattah or James's Daisy Miller; the Lady of Shallot and the Blessed Damozel are worlds away from Catherine Earnshaw. Bronte, in fact, should remind us that dead and dying women in the nineteenth century are often made of disturbing and even fearful stuff: Swinburne's women tout court, Byron's Haidee and Astarte, Scott's Ulrica, Poe's Ligeia, Rossetti's Astarte Syriaca. The destruction and death of beautiful women in the nineteenth century are all moments when the period's imaginative and cultural crises are being exposed.

In this respect later readers, particularly High Modernist readers, might reasonably judge Poe's poetry altogether too historical—even, perhaps, a reflection of the most debased kind of American Victorianism. Nor is that an unimportant way to read Poe, as Winters' essay shows. Some might take a critical view of this way of reading—as I do—because of its implicit claim to enlightenment, perhaps even historical enlightenment. However that may be, its partiality (in both senses) waylays it from access to the more significant and more difficult import of Poe's work, which calls the discourse of poetry itself to the bar of judgment. To dismiss Poe's late-Romantic posture is to miss, or perhaps refuse to accept, the troubling Platonic question it raises: What ethical authority can poetry claim when it consciously locates itself in a field of ideological illusions?

That was not just Plato's ancient question (and charge), it was also the question Whitman posed in 1875 when he found himself reconsidering his "long . . . distaste for Poe's writing.[11] A dream of Poe changed his mind.

> In a dream I once had, I saw a vessel on the sea, at midnight, in a storm. It was no great full-rigg'd ship, nor majestic steamer, steering firmly through the gale, but seem'd one of those superb little schooner yachts I had often seen lying anchor'd, rocking so jauntily, in the waters around New York, or up Long Island sound— now flying uncontroll'd with torn sails and broken spars through the wild sleet and winds and waves of the night. On the deck was a slender, slight, beautiful figure, a dim man, apparently enjoying all the terror, the murk, and the dislocation of which he was the centre and the victim. That figure of my lurid dream might stand for Edgar Poe, his spirit, his fortunes, and his poems—themselves all lurid dreams.

Whitman's dream focuses a larger set of reflections on what he called his "age's matter and malady," the "pathological" condition of "Nineteenth century . . . poetic culture." He sets Poe apart both from himself—the great apologist for the idea of a New World, the "American System"—and from "another shape of [poetic] personality,"[12]

> where the perfect character, the good, the heroic, although never attain'd, is never lost sight of, but through failures, sorrows, temporary downfalls, is return'd to again and again, and while often violated, is passionately adhered to as long as mind, muscles, voice, obey the power we call volition. This sort of personality we see more or less in Burns, Byron, Schiller, and George Sand.

Those two Romantic postures define Whitman's sense of a healthy nineteenth-century culture. Poe's difference from both is radical. With his "lurid dreams," Whitman goes on to say, he "abnegat[es] the perennial and democratic concretes" of an Age moving to a hoped-for fulfillment in the American Dream, Way, and System. Poe is unique because he does not set himself apart from "the terror, the murk, and the dislocation" of the age's "pathological" culture that Whitman himself had begun to question in *Democratic Vistas* (1871). On the contrary, he is its willing "centre and victim."

All of Poe's writing puts its readers to a test of their thinking in that political frame of reference, as scholars of the prose fiction have long understood. The politics of the poetry is less well recognized because Poe's theoretical writings seem to abjure political relation, so that we can't easily use his nonfiction prose to supply an ethical or political template for the aggressively aesthetic poetry. But in fact Poe's "unusual strings"—his poetry of intertextual appeal and suggestion—clearly anticipate the aesthetic emergency that we associate, for example, with Benjamin and Adorno. As

Jonathan Elmer has shrewdly said and shown: "Any attempt to bracket or dissipate the formalist biases of Poe's own work . . . risks de-historicizing it."[13]

We can see Elmer's point more clearly if we recur once again to Shelley and his "Defence of Poetry." Poe's work feeds upon the same nexus of cultural issues that led Shelley to call poets "the unacknowledged legislators of the world." Shelley's essay is addressing the pamphlet that his friend Thomas Love Peacock published in 1820, *The Four Ages of Poetry*. As the title suggests, Peacock's cultural critique argued that history had exposed the inconsequence of poetry to an age of Enlightenment and Modernity: "A Poet in our times is a semi-barbarian in a civilized community. He lives in the days of the past."[14] Shelley's defence counterargued that the poetic imagination was the very basis of civilization. The barbarities of the present, only too real, were not the deeds of poets but of the "anarchs" who held positions of social and political power.[15] "Poetry, and the principle of Self, of which money is the visible incarnation, are the God and Mammon of the world." For Shelley, contemporary poets—the focus of Peacock's attack—were the particular glory of an age marked by "an excess of the selfish and calculating principle":

> The cultivation of those sciences which have enlarged the limits of the empire of man over the external world, has, for want of the poetical faculty, proportionally circumscribed those of the internal world; and man, having enslaved the elements, remains himself a slave.[16]

Shelley's enslaved men will emerge later as the "beasts" of Poe's marginalium. Although Poe did not involve himself in political controversy, his mordant view of American democracy overlaps the view that Shelley shared with his critical compatriot Jeremy Bentham: "In the language of legitimacy and tyranny, and of the venal slavery that crawls under them, democracy and anarchy are synonymous terms."[17] Although readers commonly shrink from Poe's contemptuous view of American democracy, we should take it just as seriously as we take Whitman's sanguine views. As Whitman did.

Given the terms of Poe's work, however, we will do that well, I believe, only if we stay focused on Poe's aesthetic surfaces. Shelleyan politics operates in Poe under the sign of what he called "The Poetic Principle." No one doubts that Poe's musical poetics is deeply in debt to Shelley's theory of poetic imagination.[18] As we have already seen, the central paragraph of Poe's essay (paragraph 14) calls out to a key pair of Shelley's poems—"Adonais" and "One Word Is Too Often Profaned"—and carries as well a pervasive recollection of Shelley's "Defence."[19] Both men treat poetry as a discourse for exposing "the before unapprehended relations of things," or what Poe called the "combinations, and combinations of combinations."[20]

When Poe ignores Shelley's active commitment to social reform, he seems to have left poetry exposed to Peacock's principal charge of social inconsequence. In that view Poe's aestheticism isn't barbarous, it's decadent—"without the first sign of moral principle," as Whitman's phrased his initial response to Poe's writing. But then Poe's whole project redefined the poetic expression of moral principle as didactic heresy. But (then again) Yvor Winters, appalled at Poe's move, sought a further redefinition: a "poem which is a poem and nothing more" is for Winters empty and vacuous and, as such, a "catastrophe" for contemporary culture.[21]

Although Winters disapproved the content of Shelley's poetry, he did not think it contentless or ethically catastrophic. But that was his judgment of Poe's aestheticism. What Winters couldn't see, or perhaps couldn't accept, was Poe's view that only through a strict attention to poetic form can a reader experience what a poem may be saying as an appearance of truth. In this perspective, the Truth of poetry holds that all its expressions are forms of truth: appearances, illusions, and to the degree that they represent social forms, ideologies. The death of a beautiful woman is the most poetical subject in the world because that figuration, perhaps especially in the Romantic aftermath of Enlightenment, exposes the mortal limit to which poetry itself is subject.

An important change—indeed, even a "catastrophic" change— gets marked when Shelley's unacknowledged legislator consciously steps forth as the "centre and victim" of his social milieu—the beautiful and ineffectual angel of history beating his wings in vain against the storm winds of the past. So conceived, the poet reflects the emergency of his moment in the language and media of the moment. In that respect poetry's special privilege lies in the assumption it will always make: that it has no special privilege to moral or political enlightenment. This does not mean for Poe that it affirms nothing and denies nothing, or that it takes no ideological positions. Poe is not, for example, a Christian, and he often puts his "heretical" ideas on clear display—not least of all in his poetry, as we shall see shortly when we look at "The Sleeper." That he would not call his thoughts heretical is one of his more charming heresies. Poe's antididacticism is a plea to rethink the ancient idea of poetic mimesis. His argument holds that the function of poetry is to raise up a network of representations of "the good and the bad and the worst and the best" ("The City in the Sea" 3) from a vantage—in a language—that announces itself as purely representational. The writing lays bare its imaginary condition. In that move, it lays bare as well the political imaginary of a world asleep in its inheritance of illusion.

II

Consider "The Sleeper," for example, and start with an anatomy of its narrative structure.[22] Poe puts the ballad, his signature form, through many transformations from his earliest work—"Al Aaraaf" and "Tamerlane"—to his latest. Even "The Bells" tells a story. But for all their narrativity, the plots of the poems can appear simply "preposterous" or "hard to get at," like "The Raven." Accessing the story told in "The Sleeper" is a serious challenge.[23]

The difficulty becomes a foregrounded subject itself because the poem is such a clear mutation of the Sleeping Beauty legend—an extensive literary resource that is obviously cognate with the widely dispersed Beatrice legend, "the death of a beautiful woman." That vast cultural archive is the dominant feeding source for Poe's work, especially the poetry. In the case of "The Sleeper," scholars have pointed to various possible influences.[24] But like all of Poe's poetry, "The Sleeper" is such a literary echo chamber that specific identifications are less pertinent than grasping how the poem swerves from its inheritance. Tennyson's influence on Poe is especially important here: one thinks especially of his early poems "The Lady of Shalott," "The Sleeping Beauty" and its companion poem "The Arrival," "The Dying Swan," and the sleeping St. Cecily in "The Palace of Art." Such poems explicitly connect beautiful women—dead, dying, or sleeping—with beauty, art, and their place in the sordid and just-in-time world. That Tennyson was extrapolating from the same Shelleyan inheritance so important for Poe is commonplace knowledge.

But while Tennyson underscores the aesthetic politics of these legendary materials, he does not radically alter the structure of the Sleeping Beauty legend, any more than does Letitia Elizabeth Landon or other poets of that period who take it up. The core myth remains intact: that Beauty awaits the arrival of a hero, martial or theological, to set her free. Later writers, especially women bent on calling the core narrative to a revisionist political account, will move against the legend in significant ways. Angela Carter, Stevie Smith, and Helen Adam are notable. That the legend has very dark political implications sleeping within it, so to say, is perhaps most apparent from how folklore was used for internal propaganda in Nazi Germany.[25] "The Sleeper" also moves sharply against the core legend, as we see from the speaker's growing alarm that the sleep of the "lady bright" isn't "deep" enough, that it should deepen into death, so fearfully haunted is the chamber in which she lies.

The poem starts easily if also strangely: easily because a first-person narrator comes forward to set a scene for the action to come; strangely because the scene is profoundly irreal. We will shortly examine how that irreality is evoked, but for the moment we must attend to the fracturing of the narrative. Having magically appeared in the poem at the end of stanza one, Irenë—the focus of the narrator's attention—is addressed directly throughout the second stanza. The move is preposterous because Irenë, we know, "lies" sleeping "with her Destinies" (17). The line is itself preposterous because it will appear completely inexplicable when a reader first encounters it.

The narrative turns yet more obscure as stanza two develops. Poe's sleeping beauty has unaccountably moved from her resting place in the "universal valley" to an indoor "chamber" with a latticed window thrown "open to the night" "airs" (19–20).[26] Narrative obscurities multiply when the speaker suggests that the strange sleeper must have come to this place—is it even an imaginable place any longer?—"from far off seas" (32). Stanzas three and four then turn from directly addressing the lady to a prayer "to God" (42) that she might somehow move yet again, this time from her latticed chamber to a "more holy" (40) apartment. The final stanza changes the prayer to a simple hope that her "sleep" be more "deep" than any the narrator has so far imagined. He locates this within "some tall vault" in a "Far . . . forest dim and old" (48–49).

A certain local narrative order emerges following stanza two when we glimpse the rationale for the narrator's prayer to God in stanza three. The narrator prays that she might move to a chamber "more holy [and] more melancholy" (40–41) because her latticed chamber is "fearfully" (25) haunted. The move in stanza three briefly misleads us to imagine that the tale will follow a familiar, vaguely Christian, narrative line. But "the pale sheeted ghosts" (44) have not been exorcised. So at last the lady is turned over to her final resting place in stanza four. The move is in fact an Eternal Return. Irenë's last vault is not a "more holy" spot cherished by God (42) but "Some sepulchre" (54) associated with the "grand family funerals" (53) of her childhood. Resting with God—the narrative line briefly offered in stanza three—is no longer the poem's hope. Difficult as that religious rejection would be, particularly for nineteenth-century readers, more difficult still is the narrative as such, which turns startlingly particular at the end:

Some sepulchre, remote, alone,
Against whose portal she hath thrown,
In childhood, many an idle stone—
Some tomb from out whose sounding door
She ne'er shall force an echo more,
Thrilling to think, poor child of sin!
It was the dead who groaned within. (54–60)

How the narrator could possibly know about the lady's family and her childhood game of stone-throwing is not only left unexplained; the poem has made it unexplainable. Nonetheless—and this is the heart of the poetic action—the poem has told us precisely that unexplainable story by supplanting the authority of traditional narrative with the antinarrative of "Irenë, with her Destinies" (17). "The Sleeper" has not only freed her, has freed poetry, from the fate of the known Sleeping Beauty narrative, it has done this by laying out and then moving past "Irenë's two-best known legendary "Destinies": as the sleeping princess awaiting her prince in a towered chamber (stanza two) and as the sleeping soul awaiting its heavenly redemption (stanza three). Irenë's true Destiny is death, shockingly marked both as a wormy death (47) and a death from which she will utter no responsive sound. The poem ends where that other fine late poem begins: "the fever called 'Living'/ Is conquered at last" ("For Annie" 5–6).

As to death and "The Sleeper," however, Mabbott and other admiring readers find a serious problem with line 47: "Soft may the worms about her creep!" "Morbid" is the word of judgment.[27] But while the judgment is entirely just if applied to the poem's speaker—that is to say, if we read the word as a psychological marker—the judgment fails, even comically fails, if read from the point of view the poem has achieved in its final stanza. "The Sleeper" is no more authorized by its speaker than is "The Raven." Both speakers are the Everyman of antebellum America, and per-haps—if we think forward to, say, Scott Fitzgerald—of the Ameri-can Everyman tout court. Both speakers have been deranged by the experience of loss, and the poems use their narratives—the tales they tell—to track the sources of their derangement. In the speaker's experience, children of sin live in fear of the deaths that haunt their lives (ll. 59–60). In the argument of "The Sleeper," however, children of sin live in fear of the deaths that haunt their lives (ll. 59–60)—but "woe 'tis so." The poetic argument is a judg-ment on the speaker's experience, and that critical differential is everything to the poem. The sound that comes back from the stone is merely an echo from the vault's metal door. But it is a sound that also "speaks of something that is gone" forever. The speaker's Irenë—she is always his phantasm—does not want to hear the sound as such, she wants to hear it as the voice of the dead be-cause that sound would mitigate the loss, even if it would thereby also "fearfully" produce the "pale sheeted ghosts" (25, 44). Poe's poem argues against that deranged, if pitifully understandable, expectation. The dead are precious as such.

As J. T. Barbarese remarks, "the detail of the thrown stones is a surprising touch of the everyday in all this phantasmagoria, and it points to what children do all the time" (810).[28] Far from undoing the uncanny force of the poem, however, that quotidian detail pushes it across the threshold of adult illusions about the "every-day" world. It has the same effect as the move Rimbaud makes at the climactic moment of "Le bateau ivre." Rimbaud's fantastical "papillon du mai" floats in the singing "air" of Poe's fantastical June vapour. They are hearing the same unheard song in the same unimagined season.

> Si je désire une eau d' Europe, c'est la flache
> Noire et froide où vers le crépuscule embaumé
> Un enfant accroupi plein de tristesses, lâche
> Un bateau frêle comme un papillon de mai. (93–96)

> If I want a water of Europe, it is the black
> Cold puddle where in the sweet-smelling twilight
> A squatting child full of sadness releases
> A boat as fragile as a May butterfly. (trans. Wallace Fowlie)

Poe licenses a similar escape from commonplace narrative in his opening stanza, where the magical power of the legendary elixir called Nucta—unnamed in the text—generates a spacetime fit for the arrival of "Irenë, with her Destinies."

> At midnight, in the month of June,
> I stand beneath the mystic moon.
> An opiate vapour, dewy, dim,
> Exhales from out her golden rim,
> And, softly dripping, drop by drop,
> Upon the quiet mountain top,
> Steals drowsily and musically
> Into the universal valley.

The opening two lines mark the text as a kind of dreamspace where the first person speaker is part of the scene and not, as in a Romantic poem of self-expression, its composer or observer. This "I" is distinctly Rimbaudian: un autre, an element in a fantasia.

Most important, the dreamspace emerges from a pair of inter-texts.[29] Thomas Moore's *Lalla Rookh* and Shakespeare's *Macbeth* supply the "opiate vapour" that pervades the place, the time, the phenomena, the person speaking, and the unfolding of their ap-pearances.[30] Furthermore, the intertexts identify the vapour as purely magical, ethically indifferent: in Moore it is medicinal, in Shakespeare, malignant.[31] The vapour drains down through the lines, from moon to space to air to mountain and finally "Into the universal valley." That phrase (that place, that line) is the passage's astonishing summation: not a Hegelian "concrete universal" but a peculiar kind of concrete double universal, having negated that negation of imaginative vision commonly called reality.

In that move, the line finally gains the identity it would other-wise lose through didactic reference. It gains, that is, the concrete particularity of the line itself, whose unique character is defined by its startling metrical form. Six lines of steady four-stress iambs, briefly interrupted by the spondee in line seven, collapse alto-gether in a line that discovers its liberation by flaunting prosodic corruption. The line mocks all thought of normative scansion. The semantic value of its words are correspondingly shattered as the line joins together two general terms, one abstract, the other empirical. The jointure unhinges both from their general reference and binds them to a new anatomy. The consequence is most clearly marked by the term "universal," whose reference is now fixed to the semantic field of the poem. In this poetic valley, a new world is being born, whole and entire, but utterly unlike the New World of John C. Calhoun, or Henry Clay, and least of all like the imagina-tive representations springing up in the antebellum.

No one in America in 1845 is writing poetry like this, and espe-cially not in 1831 when Poe published the poem in its first version,

"Irenë."[32] "The strong sense of a beginning in Poe," Williams truly says, "is in no one else before him" (Williams 222). That he anticipates by many years much of the work we've come to canonize, not least Rimbaud's, is important to see. But that will come merely as an academic surprise, at least to many American academics. Astonishment comes when we actually look closely at the language. Poe is building palaces with the threadbare and meretricious materials of Biedermeier romanticism, the lingua franca of his epoch's cultural archive.[33] No reader understood better what Poe was doing with his language than Mallarmé. In his great tribute to Poe's poetry, the sonnet "Le Tombeau d' Edgar Poe" (1876), an angel comes to explain the purpose of Poe's linguistic "noir mélange": "Donner un sens plus pur aux mots de la tribu" (8, 6), to give a purer sense to his tribe's language. Mallarmé writes "la tribu," not "le peuple," because he knew as well as Poe that, with respect to language and culture, the savages in America were not the native Americans.

"Good workmen never quarrel with their tools": we might recall Byron's shrewd remark (*Don Juan* I. 166) when reading Poe, who accepts the tools and materials served up to him in his "magazinist" culture. We know what he thought about his epoch's beastliness, and we know how he strove to engage critically with its cultural voices. Nonetheless, he took his stand in the vulgarities of antebellum America. Did America at the time have other, fairer faces to show? Indeed it did. But then do we actually think, or want to think, that poetry only comes from or for those faces? Poe has a more tender if also a darker thought: that Books of Virtue are Books of Fear. God himself has told us so.

It is true, as the examples of Virgil and Dante insist, that great poetry can be made out of imperial and grandiose materials. It is also true that Propertius and Cecco Angiolieri were great music makers, more significant in certain ways than those more celebrated contemporaries. Like Propertius and Cecco, Poe works to save the appearances of the tawdry, the frail, the inconsequent—and even to suggest, as here, that it is dangerous to make distinctions about distinction. Yet distinctions will and should be made, as they are made here in "The Sleeper," where Christian ideology does not fare very well. But still it fares forth, full of sympathy. Cecco hated his father and wrung from his hatred several immortal poems. Certainly there is greater love than Cecco had for his father, but reading his poems we remember how often we forget the intimate relation of love and hate.

Reading "The Sleeper" Whitman might well say what he said of the American heroes he celebrated: "These so, these irretrievable" ("Song of Myself," sec. 36).[34] For in the end all is lost except what we can save in our devoted if also fractured memories. Sarah Helen Whitman—one of Poe's best readers—several times commented on Poe's "lingering pity and sorrow for the dead [and a] fear of having grieved them by some involuntary wrong of desertion or forgetfuness."[35] No critical remark ever made about Poe seems to me more incisive.

The point of Poe's great subject—"mournful and never-ending remembrance"—is to attempt the impossible: to do the dead justice on their own terms. "Annabel Lee," which I shall examine in detail below, is perhaps Poe's consummate effort to carry out that desire. But it is splendidly executed in "The Sleeper" as well, and the latter poem is particularly useful for showing how long Poe has been committed to this devotion. The child throwing stones at the vault in order to conjure an illusion of the presence of the beloved dead was the poem's final image in the poem's first (1831) version, "Irene." How fixed Poe was on that image is apparent from another poem in his 1831 volume of poems, "A Paean." This work, an early version of "Lenore," makes the connection explicit between Poe's "song" and the futile effort to cancel ultimate loss:

> Thus on the coffin loud and long
> > I strike—the murmur sent
> Through the grey chambers to my song,
> > Shall be the accompaniment. (29–32)

But what is catastrophic about this style of poetic address? As Sir Philip Sidney might say, it affirms nothing and denies nothing, it simply represents the poetic act of representation. Becoming thus a pure performative, it demonstrates to the world its social function in the world. But note that Poe has turned that demonstration into something much more troubling than the appearance of Tennyson's Lady of Shalott to the lords and dames of Camelot. Both Tennyson and Poe annotate their representations, which therefore reflect not the world but only other representations of the world—legendary intertexts and their primitive material support system, language and media. The illusions of art and poetry represent the illusions the world has always known. Poetry is thus what Poe called "A Dream (the poem) within a Dream (the world)." Poets legislate illusions from the illusions of the past. Poe and Tennyson both do this in the most self-conscious way. But there is a great difference between them. Dark as Tennyson's vision may be—the "doom of romanticism" indeed—Poe's is darker still: the doom of poetry itself, the doom of culture and its memory. Poètes et poèmes maudits.[36]

But then we must remember: poems and poets still.

The specifically critical character of Poe's demonstration is therefore doubled: on the one hand its implicit attack on the illusions of any realist or normative discourse, however sympathetic; on the other (beyond that and worse), its explicit, its performative, exposure of itself. The haunted, ominous, and fearful representations in Poe's work reflect a world living off a massive inheritance of un- or misrecognized illusions. Hence the moral of the work: those who cannot remember their illusions are condemned to pursue them, and so are those—Poe in fact—who do remember ("mournful and never-ending remembrance"). Because the memories will always be drawn from the archive of illusions, no one can escape the threat they (literally) represent.

Those who remember cherish the dead. Some—like the child in Wordsworth's "We Are Seven"—don't have to remember because the dead for them are not gone and never will be. But when the catastrophe of the beautiful occurs, when the loved become the forever lost, the official recorders of human life, the poets, plunge into crisis. Scholars, we official secondary recorders, call that crisis Romanticism and have tracked its proposals for living with the consciousness of ultimate loss. From Wordsworth to Yeats, and even beyond, comes this message of shared sympathy: "Man is in love and loves what vanishes"; "Not without hope we suffer and we mourne" (Wordsworth, "Elegiac Stanzas") The importance of Poe and Rimbaud—in fact, the reason one gets cast out and the other secedes—lies in their indifference to messages of comfort. They are primitives, like children: as adult persons they know the loved are lost, but as children they refuse to let them go—not even to that Land of Limbo, Beulahland, the realm of eternal sympathy.[37] Byron's Giaour and the wife in Frost's "Home Burial" have pledged them tormented allegiance, but so has the blithe spirit of "We Are Seven." Poe's work concelebrates the impossible marriage of a tormented and a complacent mind, but the marriage is not consummated until he writes "Annabel Lee."

Before looking closely at that culminant work, however, I want to reconsider another of Poe's notorious late works, "The Bells." This is the poem in which form is everything, the poem that perhaps more than any led Emerson to his sneering misjudgment of Poe as "The Jingle Man."

III

Larzer Ziff speaks for many readers when he remarks that "Society is scarcely depicted by Poe," who is "in flight from the social world." Poe, he says, creates "caged" and "claustrophiliac" works that promise, in lieu of society, "psychic wholeness."[38] Ziff is translating the still-dominant view of the aesthetic dimension of artistic works: in Keats's famous words, "A thing of beauty is a joy for ever." As we know, Poe's allegiance to what he called "Supernal Beauty" pivots on that imaginative assumption. But it pivots to take a sharply critical view. Far from promising psychic wholeness, Poe's works hunt down the fears lurking in that "universal valley" of illusions called by the world of getting and spending, and even by poets, "ideals." But as Mallarmé was among the first to explain, Poe's "flight from the social world" is a cunning strategy for tracking that world's flight from itself.

Stage managing such flights is the function that society assigns to its masters of illusion, the artists and the poets. When he took on the duties of that office, however, Poe came to a startling discovery. He had become himself an index of the social world he was called to represent and expose. His great French admirers immortalized Poe's discovery with a dark honorific: poète maudit. "The Conqueror Worm" is a whistle-blower's message in a bottle, Poe's most dramatic exposure of the fearful theater of art.

To bring critical assessment to his compositions—the call and response they undertake, distant screaming to battering racket—we want to shift attention from the expository features of the poetry—expressive, referential, thematic—and attend to their aesthetic and rhetorical relations. When we do that, we find ourselves in a theater of language, watching and hearing, as in "The Conqueror Worm," musical dramas. The poetry thus subordinates its possibilities of meaning to the chances of a more direct and physical experience through prosody, phonetics, and morphemics. Artful compositions, the poems make a demanding expectation for a reader performance that will reciprocate the original compositional intention.

While a poem like "The Bells" is an exacting instance of these transactions, they emerge everywhere, even (especially!) in particulars so minute they easily escape attention—like Irenë's "worms" in "The Sleeper" or—perhaps even more remarkable because more meaningless—her hair:

> Strange is thy pallor! strange thy dress!
> Strange, above all, thy length of tress (34–35)

"Strange, above all" the length of her hair?! To propose that is to estrange the word "strange," as Rimbaud recommended when he advanced his poetics of "disordering the senses." Or Blake when he wrote in "The Marriage of Heaven and Hell": "If the doors of perception were cleansed every thing would appear to Man as it is, infinite. For man has closed himself up, till he sees all things thro the narrow chinks of his cavern" (Plate 14).

When societies become caged by moral, behavioral, and religious norms—as they were for Blake, as they were for Poe and Rimbaud—poetry becomes an imperative political resort. This is so because poetry does not involve itself in the matrix of worldly illusions, where redemption comes only as another illusion. Poetry works instead to cleanse one's powers of elementary perception, the redemption of sensory experience itself, the chief inlet of soul in every age.

Poe exhibits that faith in primary imagination even in his earliest work—the "Sonnet—To Science," for example. Not a seminal poem, like "The Raven," "The Conqueror Worm," or "Ulalume." it is a work of aesthetic wit, a game he wants to play with the prosody of a foundational Western poetical form. It's a poem where we can watch Poe beginning his education in poetry, its special kind of language, and its special way of thinking. Like Science, poetry is a highly rational and analytic discourse, Poe's poetry in particular. But it is not a prescriptive discourse. It is interactive.

The game begins with the title, but readers cannot see that until they've finished reading the poem and thinking through it very carefully. With its revival in the Romantic period—Wordsworth and Keats are sonnet masters—the sonnet became a signature form of Romantic expressive poetry. Poe's sonnet fairly flaunts that recent Romantic inheritance, partly through its specific allusion to Bernardin de Saint-Pierre's "Études de la Nature," partly by directly addressing one of the period's keynote obsessions: the threat that Science was bringing to poetry.[39] Equally consequential for reading (or rereading) the poem is Poe's eclectic recovery of an earlier cultural moment. "Sonnet—To Science" is a kind of formal monster—a miscegenated construction of Petrarchan, Shakespearean, and Spenserian sonnet formalities.[40]

Poe's signature formal move, as we've seen, is to depersonalize his poetry, and his signature form of that move is to write ballads that come from an objectified narrator. These are never "realistic" characters such as we get in dramatic monologues. Like the beautiful women they love and lose, they are abstract figures, as literal as the language that creates them. All of Wallace Stevens's poetry summons just these kinds of creature. In this case, perhaps only "The Bells" comes with a speaker as literal as the one in this poem. The speaker is the Sonnet itself, who/that has come before us in his (or is it her?) full prosodic regalia. S/he is there to say something important to the poem's other, implicit character, Science.

Like Keats's Hyperion, Sonnet is in a lamentable state. An apparently greater power, a new kind of divinity, has appeared, and all Sonnet can do is upbraid Science for his (surely his) usurpation. But Poe's poem has altogether escaped that usurpation by recreating the event not as an historical or cultural truth, but as a pure aesthetic appearance. The interaction figured in Sonnet's address "to Science" turns out to refigure the relation of Poe's poem to its readers. Sonnet addresses Science, mournfully, while Poe's poem addresses its readers, playfully. The poem is the action of a Gay Science, for poetry, it turns out, can play at the game of method and technical expertise as well as Science. So we learn that there are two ways we can study Nature. One studies Nature to exploit her resources and mechanize the world. The other, the science of primary imagination, simply recreates the world as a form of truth.

"Sonnet—To Science" is an (un)seriously disorienting poem, but its very schematic character can help us negotiate Poe's two late masterpieces, "The Bells" and "Annabel Lee." I shall discuss

"The Bells" first because its problems help to clarify the general problem of Poe's poetry.

I begin with something well exposed in the reception history of "The Bells": that it has always been judged a very strange poem.[41] That quality is tracked along the three lines that shape every literary investigation: formal study, contextual analysis, and interpretation. In the best studies of poetry, these lines intersect, overlap, and are modified to suit particular cases. The reception history of "The Bells" is regularly inflected to accommodate the special character of Poe's life and work.

A good scholarly edition will display the presence of these three lines of study, as Mabbott's standard edition does. His introduction to the poem thus gives summary accounts of (1) the poem's composition, revision, and publication history; (2) the long tradition of interest in the poem as a virtuoso technical performance and an experimental challenge for one of the period's favorite pastimes, spectacular recitation; and (3) a coded representation of a landscape of psychic despair, for which Poe and his biography have always supplied both the model and the materials.

Reception history is never wrong because its full truth always remains to be seen and re-seen. This means that every reading of a poem is a true reading. Even a refusal to read is a true reading, reflecting as it does a considered judgment if not about "the poem itself" then about something seen as important and related, if only negatively, to the poem. The more readings a poem draws to itself, especially when those readings express divergent and even antithetical views, the more certain we can be of the importance of the poem. So do important poems, and poetry itself, grow inconsequent when readings coagulate and prevent a fresh engagement. So do poems and poets fall out of fashion.

In the case of "The Bells," the three general reading protocols are well established. The poem is alternatively a provocative technical exercise, a "faith destroying horror," and/or a poem that had a difficult birth and then evolved in radical ways over the better part of a year. While a pervading interest in Poe's psychology often marries interpretative and historical readings of "The Bells" (and of Poe generally), the formal issues tend to be scanted, and for very good reason. Poe's formal experiment is a mere sound of jingle bells to some, whereas to others it is the ultimate proof of Poe's craftsmanship. The history of that dividing line achieves complete definition in the case of "The Bells." Indeed, the enduring scandal of the poem marks it as prima facie a poem of the greatest importance.

But then What is it? Let us go and make our visit.

The poem was begun when Poe went to see Marie Louise Shew Houghton in New York in early 1848, sometime before May. He told her over tea that his mind and feelings were so upset by "the noise of bells tonight [that] I cannot write, I have no subject—I am exhausted."

> The lady took up the pen, and, pretending to mimic his style, wrote, 'The Bells, by E. A. Poe"; and then, in pure sportiveness, "The Bells, the little silver Bells," Poe finishing off the stanza. She then suggested for the next verse, 'The heavy iron Bells"; and this Poe also expanded into a stanza. He next copied out the complete poem, and headed it, "By Mrs. M. L. Shew," remarking that it was her poem; as she had suggested and composed so much of it. . . . He [then] slept for twelve hours.[42]

As Mrs. Houghton went on to make clear (Ingram 156), her account represents a psychological interpretation of Poe and his poetry. Arriving in a "debilitated and critical state"—"his vitality was low, he was nearly insane"—Poe is temporarily stabilized by Mrs. Houghton's friendly intervention. She helps him recover his bearings by helping him re-enter his true world, poetry. But the psychic recovery will necessarily be brief. Mrs. Houghton's good intentions were running up against the fatality of Poe, or the myth of Poe, whose poetical world is, like himself, dark and desperate.

All this is a story we know very well. It is also a true story, at once factive and mythic, as a good story should be. It also serves as documentary evidence grounding many later interpretative readings of "The Bells," not least the standard observation that the poem moves from "a world of merriment" (3) to a world of "Ghouls." Investigations into the poem's textual history then emerge with a life of their own, though they are seized by readers like Mrs. Houghton to reinforce the interpretive approach. The original poem of 17 lines expands to the finished work of 113 lines, culminating in the fourth stanza where existence is represented—in the provocative if purple words of Kenneth Silverman—"as the plaything of a lying sadistic Overlord of Life, the banquet of a Ghoul-God" (Silverman 404).

That textual history may equally turn attention to Poe the technical virtuoso. Poe will spend many months reworking the poem, completing a final version in February 1849. Here is the author of "The Philosophy of Composition" in spades. As happens regularly with Poe's work, both thematic and formal readings pick up the documentary evidence in order to fill out their respective views. But these two approaches rarely find strong points of intersection, and the documentary evidence itself is often presented as if it had no need to address seriously either the interpretative or the critical judgments. Notes on sources, echoes, and allusions keep multiplying—how could they not, Poe is a literary burglar!—but they only add to the sharp division of opinion about the poem. Is "The Bells" an experimental masterpiece or mere verse in full jingling motley? And how do we decide?

There is a neglected bibliographical feature of "The Bells" that can help to clarify both of those questions. It is in fact the poem's most arresting visible feature: the italicized word "What" that comes in lines 3, 17, 26, 38, and 72, in each case setting off the movement of each stanza. A pivotal action in the poem's visible language, it is even more important for signaling how the poem's musical structure is being organized.[43] As Christopher Aruffo has shown, Poe's critique of traditional systems of scansion in "The Rationale of Verse" centered in his argument that poetic prosody is scoring for performance, that is to say, for oral delivery and recitation.[44]

The question of the poem thus hangs upon the question of its versification. "What" is an aggressive sign to readers that the trochaic rhythm in which each stanza begins should not be allowed to slip too easily or too quickly into iambs and anapaests after lines 3, 17, 26, 38, and 72. How are we to stress, or not stress, all those otherwise insignificant prepositions and adverbs that launch so many of the poem's lines? It makes a difference whether we read line 4—and so many other lines as well—this way (following the rhythmic lead of lines 1–3, 15–17, 36–38, and 70–72):

/ ⌣ | / ⌣ | / ⌣ | /⌣
How they tinkle, tinkle, tinkle,

or this way (yielding to the unstressed invitations of all the little words that make up so many of the poem's lines):

⌣ ⌣ / | ⌣ / | ⌣ / | ⌣
How they tinkle, tinkle, tinkle,

Or consider the opening of each stanza:

> Hear the sledges with the bells—
> Silver bells!
> *What* a world of merriment their melody foretells!

> Hear the mellow wedding bells,
> Golden bells!
> *What* a world of happiness their harmony foretells!

> Hear the loud alarum bells—
> Brazen bells!
> *What* a tale of terror, now, their turbulency tells!

> Hear the tolling of the bells—
> Iron Bells!
> *What* a world of solemn thought their monody compels!

In addressing those lines, we want to recall "The Rationale of Verse," particularly Poe's comments on the problem of scanning the opening lines of Byron's "The Bride of Abydos." Readers of the passage, Poe says, have argued about its rhythm and versification because they've been deceived by traditional rules of scansion, which often put the eye at war with the ear. But, he imperiously argues, if the disputants had

> been in possession of even the shadow of the philosophy of Verse, they would have had no trouble in reconciling this oil and water of the eye and the ear, by merely scanning the passage without reference to lines, and, continuously, thus:
>
> Know ye the | land where the | cypress and | myrtle Are | emblems of | deeds that are | done in their | clime Where the | rage

of the | vulture the | love of the | turtle Now | melt into | softness
now | madden to | crime (CT 106)

And so forth. For Poe, scansion must be true to "the customary accentuation" of words as they are actually spoken so that "The rhythmical must agree, thoroughly, with the reading, flow" (ibid. 107). Everything about poetic rhythm and its underlying music for Poe resolves into recitation: how the poetry is to be performed by the "reading" individual.

But the "reading flow" of "The Bells" is anything but a foregone thing. The poem is so organized that its readers are constantly presented with difficult and consequential performance alternatives.[45] "*What*" puts the reader on notice that recitation decisions have to be made that will materially affect the meaning of the poem. Of special importance, for instance, is the word "How" (lines 4, 19, 27, 28, 40, 54, 64, 74). How indeed do the different bells sound, and how are these lines to be sounded? Or in the case of the wedding bells, for example, how does their "euphony" "swell"? "How it dwells/ On the Future" is commonplace in a simple expository sense, but if we strongly stress that word "How" in line 28, other less simple meanings begin to be suggested.

"Danger ebbs and flows" in the music of this poem, but how does that happen, and how do we know it? Poe tells us how:

How the danger ebbs and flows:—
Yes, the ear distinctly tells,
    In the jangling,
    And the wrangling,
How the danger sinks and swells, (60–64)

In this poetic world, the ear hears more, and the eyes see more, than the mind can process or the heart can know. While the words *"What"* and "How"—the sounding of those words—are strong determiners of the poem's meanings, they pressure all their immediate subordinates—all of the other first words in each line of the poem—to have their sound values declared. The declarations can only be made by readers.[46] In this respect, consider in the fourth stanza the words "They" (86–88) and "And" (79, 82, 89, 90, 92, 94). What is at stake comes out with great clarity in this passage:

> They are neither man nor woman—
> They are neither brute nor human,
>   They are Ghouls:—
> And their king it is who tolls:—
> And he rolls, rolls, rolls, rolls,
>   A Pæan from the bells!
>   And his merry bosom swells
>   With the Pæan of the bells! (86–93)

If in reading/recitation we stress those three "Ands," the meaning of the "melancholy menace" (75) of the iron bells greatly augments. Correlatively, so much depends on how we read/recite the sequence "They are . . . They are . . . They Are": as trochees, as iambs, as spondees, or as some combination of those options, and how we stress (or not) the first words of these lines. Especially interesting (to me) is the scansion of line 88 ("They are Ghouls"), which runs a prosodic rhyme with lines 71, 78, 81, and 98. In those four instances the second syllable is clearly unstressed. The presence of those lines thus throws into relief the various options for reading/reciting line 88: "They are Ghouls." All three words in the line could easily bear recitation stress, but alternatives are plainly available, not least a sequence of stressed syllables with stress modulations.

The poem is a challenge to meaning because it is a challenge to recitation. In every line, readers face consequential decisions that will affect the meaning of the poem. What does one do with line 50, for example: "By the side of the pale-faced moon"? Or with those repeating lines that repeat the word "bells," which clearly run to an ominously long-drawn-out time because of the word's heavily voiced consonants.[47] For that matter, how do we read lines 46–50? Do they link to the "deaf and frantic fire," surely one's first thought? Or are they perhaps running in apposition with lines 44–45 and thus referencing the shrieking bells. Playing tricks with syntax by playing off the prosody is a game poets, Poe especially, play all the time. Those games expose Poe's fundamental "Poetic Principle," that poetry's mortal music runs an "upper current" of meaning that allows us to glimpse an "under current" of more capacious meanings, though all the meanings will fall short of the encompassing harmony that the poetry desires to reach. In the first stanza, for example, the "Silver bells—or perhaps "the stars," or perhaps "the heavens," or perhaps all three—are

> Keeping time, time, time,
> In a sort of Runic rhyme,
> To the tintinabulation that so musically wells
> From the bells, bells, bells, bells,
> Bells, bells, bells— (9–12)

We will not hear that "sort of Runic rhyme" again until we're far into the last stanza, where it is associated with the time of Silverman's "sadistic Overlord of Life." Like the subject matter taken up in nearly all of Poe's important poems, this begins in Illusion and ends in Fear, which is the great truth of Silverman's reading. But that relation of Poe's poem to its metallic subject reminds us that the work is keeping the time of two different temporalities: one rules the sublunary world of "The good and the bad and the worst and the best" ("The City in the Sea" 4), which is the world as well of poets and their poetry. But there is another world of "Supernal" music overruling that sublunary world. To that world all poets and poetry are bound by faith and desire—all of them, "the good and the bad and the worst and the best" alike. It is the cool template by which we are able to see more clearly our world of illusion and torment.

So the key phrase "What a world" has a double reference. It is also semantically double jointed. We don't know what the double world of "The Bells" is, but we do know it is breathtaking. "The Bells," it seems, is not a *what* at all, except poetically. It is more like a *how* since it can only be accessed through musical action—the poem's harmony, the reader's subsequent, reciprocal performance—and it is meant for a music lesson. The lesson is sent to a world needing clear access to the beguiling, distracting, alarming, and finally horrifying noise of bells. It needs such access in order to realize what it needs even more: music, supernal beauty.

The poem's music turns four types of bell to instances of sounds that, except for poetry, would untune the sky. The sound of bells is not the sound of music. It is the sound of the quotidian world—"The battering racket about him"—whereas music is the unheard sound of poetry. That is the argument of "The Bells," and the performance of the poem is the argument's proof. But circumstantial evidence can help us recognize both. The story of Poe's physical and mental distress on the day the poem was begun has served that function for a long time. Here is another interesting circumstantial fact: that a memory of De Quincey, one of Poe's favorite authors, is attending upon the poem's most notorious word, "tintinnabulation." *The Confessions of an English Opium-Eater* (1821) has the following passage—it can speak for itself—in which De Quincey recalls his torment-by-bells when he was at Oxford:

> The persecutions of the chapel-bell, sounding its unwelcome summons to six o'clock matins, interrupts my slumbers no longer, the porter who rang it . . . is dead, and has ceased to disturb [those] who suffered much from his tintinnabulous propensities. . . . The bell . . . rings, I suppose, as formerly, thrice a-day, and cruelly annoys, I doubt not, many worthy gentlemen, and disturbs their peace of mind; but as to me, in this year 1821, I regard its treacherous voice no longer (treacherous I call it, for, by some refinement of malice, it spoke in as sweet and silvery tones as if it had been inviting one to a party); its tones have no longer, indeed, power to reach me . . . for I am 250 miles away from it, and buried in the depth of mountains. And what am I doing among the mountains? Taking opium. ("Introduction to the Pains of Opium")

Poe's poem served him much as De Quincey was served by his mountain retreat. But then what of us, the poem's readers? Why has Poe made such a problem of the versification of "The Bells," why disorder its prosodic senses as he has so clearly done? My answer would be: to disorder our senses and by that to wake his neighbors up at our most elementary level of human attention. "The Bells" asks us to make decisions, actual choices, about how to articulate its language, and then to notice, or realize, what those choices tell us about ourselves. For our recitations will reflect our understandings and hence of our world. Williams says that "The whole period, America 1840, could be rebuilt, psychologically . . . from Poe's [aesthetic] method" (231), and that is both true and important. But equally true and important is how the method was devised for promiscuous interpretive performance. "The Bells" invites each reader to a deliberated engagement with something that appears inconsequent and even simple: an articulated reading of a poem. But the invitation is full of import and consequence since we will inevitably find the task seriously demanding. A bad recitation of "The Bells" will have lost all contact with the supernal beauty its music celebrates. It will simply be a jingling and jangling of what Whitman called "the age's [in this case, our age's] matter and malady," not a poetic diagnosis—which is what he wanted.

Actions speak louder than words, and when poetry is at stake, recitation is more dangerous, because more defenseless, than interpretation. For what should we think if, faced with a test as apparently inconsequent as poetic recitation, we find ourselves weighed in the balance of a little poem and found sorely wanting? Would our incompetence frighten us? Or would it be more fearful yet if we weren't frightened at all?

IV

"Annabel Lee" has a special importance in Poe's oeuvre partly because it was his last poem, and partly because it delivers his final, perhaps even summary, treatment of "the death of a beautiful woman." In resuming that notorious topic, Poe veered decisively from the rhetoric of the poems that preceded "Annabel Lee." "The Raven," "The Sleeper," "Lenore," and "Ulalume" all begin in Illusion and end in Fear. Equally, the affective shape of those poems is a function of their explicitly nonsubjective character: "Lenore" is a balladic dialogue, and the other three are not only "spoken" by narrators, the narrators are clearly unbalanced (as the lover in "Lenore," though bitter toward Lenore's false "friends," is not). That impersonal poetic mode, as we've seen, allows Poe to run his characteristic double music, the poetic under current working against the threats and fears that Poe's narrators bear along the upper currents of the verse.

A nonsubjective approach to "Annabel Lee" is certainly possible, though it would work against the autobiographical approaches that have prevailed from its first publication. These not only dominate the poem's early reception history, they also exploit its unusual affective address. Given the poem's signature topic, the tone of "Annabel Lee" is strikingly untroubled, as if Poe had finally escaped what Blake called "the Torments of Love and Jealousy."[48] But whether the poem's form is taken as subjective or impersonal, "Annabel Lee" does not appear to solicit the Catastrophe of Beauty. Fear seems absent from the poem's conclusion.

If we suppose the speaker is a narrator in the line of the earlier poems, however, we might argue that his sorrow has turned his fear catatonic. This reading could be supported by pointing to an interesting textual fact: the two most authoritative witness texts add the words "A Ballad" to the title. If we want evidence for an unbalanced narrator we need only read the poem, especially the last four lines, alongside attitudes toward death and mourning that prevail now. In such a perspective those final lines may well appear, as they have been called, "macabre," "compulsive," "bizarre," "pathological," "morbid."[49] Historicist scholars, however, argue that whatever we might think today about those lines, Poe's contemporaries would have read them as thoroughly conventional nineteenth-century American memorializing.[50] While that view of Poe's poem is inaccurate in certain important ways, as we shall see, it points to a signal truth about the poem: that early sympathetic readers did not read it as a scene of psychic derangement. For them, "Annabel Lee" was Poe's perfected expression of an ideal and absolute love.

If we then shift our vantage to Poe and his manifest intentions, the problem of interpretation becomes even more interesting and difficult. For all the received lines of reading pursue thematic and ethical ends. Poe's sympathetic contemporaries found as much cultural value in the "love that was more than love"—as they understood it—as readers have recently found in subverting such an idea of love, or in historicizing it as congruent with a contemporary "culture of mourning." But these interpretive approaches are all, from Poe's perspective, didactic heresies. They argue that the poetry can, perhaps should, represent ideas and convictions that have some kind of normative presence and authority. It is as much a moral decision to say of the speaker of "Annabel Lee" that his love is "macabre" as that it is "natural, simple, tender, and touchingly beautiful."[51] These candles held up in the sunshine of the poem are less important as reflections *on* the poetry than as reflections *of* prevailing social norms.

Nonetheless, they still have real importance as reflections on the poetry, and therefore also on their status as social norms. They prove—I should rather say, the entire archive of readers and readings prove—that poetry is exactly as promiscuous as Plato regretfully thought it was. "To what serves mortal beauty?" Gerard

Manley Hopkins asked in his sonnet so titled, and Poetry answers: it will serve the desires of anyone who will pay . . . attention. In return—this is ancient wisdom—poetry holds up a mirror where we may reflect on reflections of nature and the world. Poe comes to annotate that truth by adding: since we are nature and the world, poetry holds the mirror up to us, giving us back our own image and likeness, whether we like it or not. To most early readers, the thought that "Annabel Lee" is "macabre" would itself have seemed a deeply macabre thought.

The Catastrophe of Beauty in Poe's work thus takes two general forms. One is a great form of Fear, the sum of all fears that preyed upon Poe and his world. And of that fearful world we should remember what Thomas Hardy later told God: "Lord, it existeth still" ("God-Forgotten"). The second, a form of Knowledge, may also take a form of Fear. It is poetry's confession of self-knowledge, which for Poe also means a clear declaration of its limits. Poetry represents the irritable, because perpetually thwarted, reaching after fact, reason, and "Supernal Beauty." Perhaps with "Annabel Lee," then, Poe is making peace with the poet's limit conditions. If one compares "Annabel Lee" with "Lenore," which tells virtually the same story, the tonal difference between the poems is striking. The speaker of "Lenore" rails against the "Wretches" (8) who lament Lenore's death, and when he finally declares that his "heart is light" (20), his words are still defiant. But in "Annabel Lee," those tense emotions are gone.

Unlike the earlier poems treating the death of a beautiful woman, "Annabel Lee" exposes the source of those tensions in terms that Poe would himself recognize as legitimate: that is, intertextual and aesthetic terms. That difference marks the special position "Annabel Lee" holds in Poe's corpus. More than any of his poems, with the possible exception of "The Conqueror Worm," "Annabel Lee" makes a lurid dream of Western poetry's most important illusion of transcendence: the Dantean myth of Beatrice.

It works toward exposing that myth from the outset. The opening lines establish the poem's fabulous character ("It was many and many a year ago/ In a kingdom by the sea" = "Once upon a time in a land far, far away"). Because that formulaic move is so self-conscious, readers are encouraged to make current applications, to bring the story down to a time, place, and people "you may know" (3). Here the allusions concealed in the title can help. The poem suggests that we may well know who Annabel Lee is, and Poe's contemporary readers might perhaps know even better than we. Her name conflates the names of Byron's first wife, Annabella, and his beloved sister, Augusta Leigh. Byron was famously "dissevered" (32) from both and in 1849 those separations were still uncomplicated emblems of lost romantic love, of which Byron was the age's chief index.[52] This kingdom by the sea thus opens out from America to England and perhaps to even more extensive global connections.

But such a reading of the title, while attractive, is also difficult because it isn't insistent. It's just "suggestive," as if to suggest: he who has ears to hear, let him hear. Much more insistent are certain details in the poem's four central stanzas where the story of the lovers is sketched. Here we aren't dealing with a possible or suggestive intertext but with one that seems quite certain. Indeed, nowhere else in Poe's many treatments of the death of a beautiful woman is the western source of that myth more clearly recalled.

We track it to Dante and Petrarch, to Beatrice and Laura. Beatrice is the ultimate model, however, and Dante tells her story in his *Vita Nuova*. The key texts in that work are the three great canzoni: "Donne ch'avete intelletto d'amore" ("Ladies that have intelligence in love"), "Donna pietosa e di novella etate" ("A very pitiful lady, very young"), and "Gli occhi dolenti per pietà del core" ("The eyes that weep for pity of the heart"). In these poems Dante first anticipates, then dreams of, and finally reflects after the fact upon the untimely death of Beatrice.[53]

That "Annabel Lee" is referencing those poems by Dante seems beyond question, though, remarkable to say, it has not been pointed out before. The core narrative in Poe's ballad and the *Vita Nuova* both arrange an equivalent set of characters and events. "A love that was more than love" erupts magically when the lovers are mere children: Dante falls in love with Beatrice when they are both about nine years old, and in Poe the lovers' mutual devotion has existed since "*She* was a child and *I* was a child,/ In this kingdom by the sea" (7–8). The perfection of that love (in Poe) and the perfection of the beloved (in Dante) is so great that it drives various transmortal beings, including God, to separate the lovers by taking the beloved away. The loss of the beloved in each case utterly transforms the lovers, finally driving both beyond the framework of the ordinary world.

But of course Dante's story and Poe's finally move in radically different directions. Most strikingly, Beatrice is taken up to heaven while Annabel Lee is killed and entombed "in a sepulchre there by the sea" (40). That skew between the two stories reflects the sharp difference in the initiating set of events: Beatrice is drawn heavenward by the perfect desire of God and his heavenly host, whereas

Annabel Lee is killed because transmortal beings "coveted" (12) the lovers' devotion for each other. Poe's word recalls only to pollute the original Dantescan scene and event. As for the end of the tales, Dante's loss awakens his passion to join Beatrice in heaven and the embrace of God's transcendent love. Annabel Lee's lover desires only to "lie down by the side" of his dead beloved forever. The desire is expressed grammatically in what Gertrude Stein would call a "continuing present," mortalized *in saecula saeculorum* ("And so all the night-tide, I lie down by the side" (38)).

That Poe's poem appears to sustain its Dantescan references only to deconstruct its theological myth is striking. In each case the issue is transmortal love: Poe's "love that is more than love" (im)perfectly mirrors Dante's transcendent love. Poe is, as Charles Bernstein might say, "Recalculating" Dante, and if we review some of the key points of contact the move seems unmistakable.[54] Dante's first canzone, for example, imagines a dialogue in heaven about Beatrice between God and his angels. It is a subject that will reach down even to the "accurst that writhe" in hell (27). All the citizens of heaven, saints and angels, are so struck by her perfection that they long for her presence ("Madonna in the empyrean is desired" 29). But God tells them to be patient because He is aware that Dante, who dreads "her loss," has a great poetical mission in his future, the composition of the *Commedia*:

> My well-beloved, suffer now in peace
> That she you hope for, while my pleasure is,
> Should still abide where one awaits her loss
> Who to the accursed crew in hell shall say,
> The hope of blessed spirits I have seen. (24–28)

189

By the time of the third canzone, however, Beatrice has died, "gone to yonder heaven" (15) because God himself now desires her real presence. Her splendor is such

> As woke amaze in the Eternal Sire,
> And kindled sweet desire
> To call a soul so lovely to his rest.
> Then made he it from earth to him aspire,
> Deeming this life of care and sorrowing
> Unworthy of so fair and pure a thing. (23–28)

This congruence between Dante's tale of Beatrice and Poe's story of Annabel Lee is important, but the relation becomes irresistible when we note that Poe's cloud in stanza three (line 15)—a signal device in the story of Annabel Lee's killing—is taken straight from Dante's second canzone:

> I raised the eyes then, moistened with my tears,
> And softly as the shower of manna fell,
> Angels I saw returning up to heaven;
> Before them was a slender cloud extended,
> And from behind I heard them shout, Hosanna.[55] (57–61)

One further textual congruence is equally striking: when Annabel Lee is taken from her lover, Poe stresses the word "chilling" to describe the event. The same word comes into Dante's third canzone, though the application is significantly different:

> No icy chill or fever's heat deprived
> Us of her, as in nature's course;
> But solely her transcendent excellence. (18–20)

In Poe, Annabel Lee is chilled to death by "A wind [that] blew out of a cloud by night" (14). In Dante, this is the cloud that God sent down to earth as the vehicle for Beatrice's trip to heaven. In Poe it is a cloud of covetous envy, "chilling and killing."

These Dantean references multiply our interpretive problems with the poem. At first the problem is strictly historical. How and when did Poe access Dante's poems? Readers have not perhaps noticed Poe's use of Dante because he never mentions the *Vita Nuova* and probably never read it. His Italian would have been inadequate to the task. Besides, the first complete English translation did not appear until 1846 and then only in Florence in an edition that seems to have been almost completely unknown, and is today an exceedingly rare volume.[56] Certainly it was not known to the three men whose own notable translations were being undertaken in the 1840s and 1850s (none of which would appear until well after Poe's death). It's true that Poe could have read Charles Lyell's translations of the *canzonieri*, which include the three *canzoni* that stand at the center of the *Vita Nuova*. Lyell published those translations in 1836 and his book was reprinted in 1840. Another set of translations of the *Vita Nuova*'s poetry, perhaps less accessible to Poe, appeared in *Tait's Magazine* in 1845. But Poe never hints an acquaintance with these works either in his prose or in any of his earlier Beatricean poems.

The obscurity about Poe's source texts is not just a pedantic problem for scholarship. Because Dante's work gets so explicitly recuperated in "Annabel Lee," one wonders why it has no presence in the earlier Beatricean poems. The stories in "Lenore" and "Annabel Lee" are nearly identical, but Lenore does not reference Dante's story.[57] Did Poe not know about the *Vita Nuova* poems until very late? Or if he was aware earlier of the story and the poems, did he deliberately conceal his recalculations of Dante until 1848? And if so, why the initial concealment or, for that matter, why the final exposure?

Whatever the case, Poe's move against Dante puts enormous pressure on the key line "But we loved with a love that was more than love" because the traditional model for such a love is so clearly Dantescan. But Poe seems to have called Annabel Lee from the tomb of Dante in the same spirit that moved Wallace Stevens to call Badroulbadour from the tomb of the *Arabian Nights*.[58] Poe and Stevens are each preoccupied with what Stevens will call "the worms at heaven's gate" because a traditional gatekeeper like Dante expelled all "wormy circumstance" from his poems about Beatrice.[59]

But then nearly all readers also seem bent upon casting out the worms, not least our contemporary critics of Poe's "macabre" imagination. Mrs. Frances Osgood's reading, which typifies the best that was known and thought about the poem in the nineteenth century, certainly meant to cast them out as well. But she casts them out in a modified Dantescan spirit when she calls the poem "natural, simple, tender and touchingly beautiful." Though she never mentions Dante or Beatrice, Mrs. Osgood evidently read the poem in a spirit of Christian Platonism that she could accommodate to her nineteenth-century sentimental response to

the beautiful meaning latent in the most lovely of all
[the poem's] verses—where he says,

"A wind blew out of a cloud, chilling
My beautiful Annabel Lee,
So that her high-born kinsmen came,
And bore her away from me."

There seems a strange and almost profane disregard of the
sacred purity and spiritual tenderness of this delicious
ballad, in thus overlooking the allusion to the *kindred
angels* and the heavenly *Father* of the lost and loved and
unforgotten wife.[60]

Nothing about the poem would be "macabre" for Mrs. Osgood,
any more than the worms in "The Sleeper" would be "morbid." To
our contemporaries, however, a cultural-critical and historicist
perspective exposes the limitations of both Dantescan transcendental idealism and nineteenth-century sentimental idealism.
Contemporary readers who find the poem "macabre" bring critical
enlightenment to Poe's poem and its nineteenth-century "culture
of mourning."

What is the love that is more than love if it isn't divine love (traditionally understood)? The answer I suppose is simple and obvious: it is some kind of human love, but somehow made more
perfect than it often appears. In the case of "Annabel Lee," an "exquisite pathos" became available to readers when they identified
such perfection with Poe's love for his wife Virginia. And surely if
we now cannot sympathize with Mrs. Osgood's faith in that kind
of love, frail as it might seem to much current thinking about love
and marriage, we will have difficulty sympathizing with the poem.
(Since many *do* have difficulty sympathizing with the poem in
that perspective, "subversive" readings emerge.) I cite Mrs. Osgood here because, far more than many of our contemporaries,
"exquisite pathos" is a fair response to the tone and affect of "Annabel Lee."

For catastrophe is the price that Eternity sets for "the love that
is more than love." Blake called it "The price of Experience":

"What is the price of Experience? Do men buy it for a song?
   Or wisdom for a dance in the street? No, it is bought with
     the price
   Of all that a man hath. . . ."   (The Four Zoas, Night the Second)[61]

In Poe's case, the price is sentimentally—fearfully—figured as "my darling—my darling—my life and my bride." For "It is an easy thing to rejoice in the tents of prosperity," where "the groan and the dolour are quite forgotten." But when God and his angels, saints, and devils conspire to separate Poe's lovers, an unforeseen chance opens to turn the debacle to account. The poem now poses a question: will that disastrous wrong be met by a correspondent "wrong of desertion or forgetfulness"? Reading the poem's final lines, who will not experience the desire for such a starry flight from the "sepulchre there by the sea"?

However we negotiate the ethics of that finale, however we *feel* about it, the formal logic of the poem identifies it with "the love that is more than love." In dismantling the traditional myth of Beatrice, then, Poe is in effect re-interpreting the myth of the Fall. In Poe's story, if there is an Original Sin it is committed by transmortal beings, including God himself, who introduce Death into the lovers' world out of "envy" for an unimaginable love. In Poe's poem, the love of one frail mortal person for another frail mortal person throws the perfect love of God into a critical perspective. Paradoxically, the move to destroy this mortal love ends with its complete realization. The "love that is more than love" is exceptional not merely because it is doomed to loss and death but because it embraces that unredeemable condition. The lover's sepulchral choice in effect marks a transvaluation of the traditional order of mortal/immortal values, and the poem's complacent affect identifies what we can truly call a peace that passeth understanding. Indeed, so far surpasses that it can appear—does appear—ghoulish, so powerful is the ideology of transcendence.

In that respect, we can hardly doubt the success of the poem's argument, which tests the sympathetic capacities of sentimental and skeptical readers alike. "Exquisite pathos" seems as apt a critical comment as one could make for a poem that tells such a tale. But we have to be careful not to confuse the import of the final four lines—*what* is happening—with their tone—*how* it is being represented. The complacency is the sign of the presence of the upper music. Poe was hardly unaware of the fear and horror that Death engendered, or of the ways people never cease trying what is in fact impossible (as impossible as the desire of the moth for the star): to mitigate, conquer, or escape Death, to realize transcendence. "Macabre" is therefore in its own way another thoroughly apt comment on the final lines. It shows that the poem can't be read without registering the "chill"—the Fear and Loathing—that surrounds our experience of Death.

Mrs. Osgood's sympathetic effort to meet the poem's tone would mean nothing if a sense of the macabre and pathological had no presence even for her. Though "Exquisite pathos" is a term of sympathy, it is also discounted and equivocal, as if Mrs. Osgood wanted to protect the poem from possible misconstruction, as in fact she did.[62] In an important sense, "exquisite pathos" and "macabre" are obverse and reverse of a view that has registered the alienation of the poem's central positions: that the transmortal world has "coveted" the childlike lovers and finally killed Annabel Lee, and that her lover's response is to join her in the earthy death to which a divine order has decided to condemn her. That envy-driven order is reversed when the lover makes his suicidal decision to rejoin her.

These poetic representations don't suit themselves to orthodox or unorthodox Christian ideas prevalent in nineteenth-century America.[63] As for later readers, "Annabel Lee" offers only complacencies of the *Poe noir*. So the Dantescan lexicon places the poem in a foundational Western ideological context that readers keep struggling to accommodate. "Exquisite pathos," "macabre," and "pathological" are as much historical comments and political judgments as they are ethical and psychological. To see the narrator as catatonic—a clearly available view—underscores the alienation that the poem counter-covets.

One other feature of "Annabel Lee" is relevant: its prosody. Unlike "The Bells," the versification of "Annabel Lee" does not issue a clear challenge to performative interpretation. The rhythm is firmly anapaestic in alternating tetrameter and trimeter lines, with some important variations especially in the opening foot. A good example of sophisticated podic verse, its upper rhythmic currents pledge allegiance to folk metres and nursery rhyme. This familiar prosody argues that the ballad is telling a simple and familiar story, and the poem fairly encourages a careless sing-song reading. But if the original story is indeed familiar and longstanding, its alienated treatment produces that rhythmic under current—the unheard melody—that Poe made the chief object of poetry.

Crucially, the poem does not demand recitations that might deviate from the insistent podic form. "Annabel Lee" does not work like "The Bells," and its unheard melody is no different in appearance from the upper current of its verse. The poem's argument depends upon maintaining that apparitional congruence.

Unlike "The Raven" and "Lenore," "Annabel Lee" is not constructed to expose an imaginative division (between narrator and poet, between fiendish friends and lover). Its "sweet" versification therefore mirrors its inmost self, its music. But if the versification is not at odds with its music, the poem does appear seriously at odds with the myth of Beatrice as constructed in Dantescan terms. The poem's tonal complacency thus stands against the heartless ethos brought to earth from the tormented regions of hell and heaven.

In that perspective, the question of "Annabel Lee"—the question of its performance, of its meaning as performance—might well be judged far more difficult than the same question posed by "The Bells," where readers are encouraged to experiment with its performative meanings. "Annabel Lee" has laid down a far more stringent prosodic demand: to find a performative means for representing the lover's position as simultaneously simple, innocent, and childlike as well as perverse, unseemly, even monstrous.

The collision of those demands is both the consummation and the catastrophe of the poem. It is to have imagined something impossible *as impossible*, and then to have proposed it as necessary. If as Charles Bernstein wittily suggests, that "A thing of beauty is annoyed forever," it is also the case that things of beauty, like lively and difficult children, will and should annoy for ever.[64] Who would have it otherwise? Not Jesus, not even Wordsworth. "Annabel Lee" will annoy forever the myth of Beatrice, which is itself so splendidly annoying (who would have it otherwise?).

Poe always knew that the death of a beautiful woman was the most poetical subject in the world. In "Annabel Lee" he remembers why he knew that. It is a truth pervading his (and our) cultural memory, a mythic understanding as fundamental to Western consciousness as the myth of Faust. Dante had realized the idea in *La Vita Nuova*, where he created a new life for poetry in vernacular language out of the discourse of Christian eschatology. But when "Annabel Lee" remembers that Dantescan inheritance, it recovers its entirety, as Keats had done in his sonnet on Paolo and Francesca. At the core of the myth is the experience of pain, sin, and loss that cannot be mitigated. Equally at its core is the experience of that experience. Philosophy and religion translate that secondary experience as, alternatively, self-consciousness and divine faith. In doing so, philosophy and religion shift the pain, sin, and loss to a redemptive mode. That shift does not happen in poetry, certainly not in Poe (or—to take an analogous case—in the sonnet where Keats also re-engaged the Beatricean myth, "A Dream, After Reading Dante's Episode of Paolo and Francesca"). In poetry, the experience is imitated or modeled in the entirety of its impossible contradiction.

That is what happens in "Annabel Lee" when Poe refigures the myth of Beatrice. "Annabel Lee" lifts up an impossible love against Dante's imaginative illusion, the Beatricean myth of transcendent love. Poe's is not a travesty of Dante; it recomposes Dante in a new, secular key; and the result is not a cultural myth of redemption but a redemption of Dante, and of poetry itself, lest the didactic heresies that all poetry necessarily traffics in be taken for its truth.

Given Poe's poetics, that move shifts our attention from the heresies to the prosody, where Poe's outrageous new figurations are carried along what appears a tensionless surface. The question of the poem then becomes not what it *means* but how we are to register its music—in fact, how we are to perform that music, how we are to recite the poem. "The Bells" coded into itself explicit instructions for adventurous recitation, but "Annabel Lee" abandons us to what prosodists call its "sweet" versification, as if the poem's suicide mission were the easiest thing to imagine or execute.[65] All the received readings of the poem, including the hostile ones, remind us of the poem's drive toward—its commitment to—a masculine suttee.

That situation leaves us with two general recitation procedures. We can yield entirely to Poe's sweet versification and produce the kind of "sing-song" reading that Coleridge recommended for children in *Biographia Literaria*.[66] This would be a reading such that all the evil in the poem, including the evil that Poe visits upon the myth of Beatrice, is made subject to a childlike innocence. The demonic intentions of God, angels, and devils are not removed from the poem—far from it—but they are rendered less consequent than the musical innocence that opposes them, the love that is more than the love driving the myth of heaven and hell. In this way do we understand, after Shelley (and Poe), that "Our sweetest songs are those that tell of saddest thought" ("To a Skylark").

Alternatively, we can disregard Coleridge's instructions for performance and follow what he saw as a "prose" rendering of the metrical contract. Coleridge explicitly associated this procedure with Wordsworth's idea that "There neither is, nor can be, any essential difference between the language of prose and metrical composition" ("Preface" to *Lyrical Ballads*). Vehemently disagreeing with that view and the poetic practice it licensed, Coleridge took it as the "chief inducement" for his strictures on Wordsworth in *Biographia Literaria*, which is exactly where he promoted his instruction for a "sing-song" response to poetic recitation. But Wordsworth's would prove to be a revolutionary poetical move, laying the ground for everything we now understand as Modern Poetics. Wordsworth recognized that a poetical composition necessarily puts into play two rhythmic orders, one artfully deployed as a decisive "metrical composition," the other as the fatefully declared music of vernacular language, our Mother Tongue. A vernacular recitation of "Annabel Lee" will recompose the verse according to what Paull Baum called "the other harmony of prose," lest we forget how deep a discordance lurks at the heart of "our sweetest songs."[67] Medieval theologians called that lurking discordance *diabolus in musica*.

In that respect we might see in Poe's little poem its under current of critical reflection on poetry's social function: to put us at our dis-ease. Crucially, to put us at our dis-ease in the little realm of poetry itself. For the world of getting and spending keeps tempting us—keeps tempting poets especially—to imagine how to escape the world of injustice and loss, a seductive idea that serves so well the princes of that world. "Annabel Lee" is far from an "escapist" poem, as its final "macabre" imagining insists. Nor was Baudelaire's poem "Any where out of the world" issuing a call to flee. It was a cry of pain, an index of what it means to be the "center and victim" of the world we ourselves have made and keep making. At its best, poetry will keep up its simulations of all we have done and keep doing, all of "The good and the bad and the worst and the best." "But woe 'tis so," as our sweetest singers have made it their vocation to remind us.

Coda

✍

> ... sounds tormenting the ear and yet stimulating
> the imagination and stirring the soul ...
>
> (Michel Fokine on Stravinsky's *Petrushka*)

I began this study of Poe by looking at some of his representative *Marginalia*. Because those texts display Poe's implacable self-consciousness, they reflect the two distinctive qualities of his writing, and especially his poetry: its intelligence and its arresting surface effects. Like Tennyson (whom Poe thought the greatest poet of the age) and Swinburne (who thought Poe "the complete man of genius"), the poetry does not take its richly embodied forms from any natural things.[1] Poe's work is the artifice of mortality.

Another marginalium—a late one—is worth considering here since it echoes and seems to qualify "The Philosophy of Composition," Poe's manifesto for artistic self-consciousness.

> To see distinctly the machinery—the wheels and pinions—of any work of Art is, unquestionably, of itself, a pleasure, but one which we are able to enjoy only just in proportion as we do *not* enjoy the legitimate effect designed by the artist:—and, in fact, it too often

201

happens that to reflect analytically upon Art, is to reflect after the fashion of the mirrors in the temple of Smirna, which represent the fairest images as deformed. (*Marginalia* July 1849)[2]

Recall that he opens "The Philosophy of Composition" with an ironical reflection on Romantic sincerity. Because "Most writers—poets in especial—prefer having it understood that they compose by a species of fine frenzy," Poe observes, they "would positively shudder at letting the public take a peep behind the scenes, at the . . . wheels and pinions" that constitute the machinery of composition. Proud of his commitment to craftsmanship, Poe then creates a theatrical representation of the process of poetic invention. As Mallarmé was the first to understand, the essay is more a prose poem than a critical exegesis. It is a display of imaginative invention carried out not merely in a prose medium, but in a prose that affects an informational and declarative posture.

Readers of Poe—not all, but some of the best—have been dazzled by these games of aesthetic virtuosity. The writing is performative throughout and feeds upon its self-displays. But those are far from the principal object of the poetry, as Poe reminds us in this late marginalium. Beyond the "pleasure" we take in a spectacle of poetic mastery lies "the legitimate effect designed by the artist," the reader's experience of the "fleeting" presence of "Supernal Beauty." This appears as the artifice of mortality that Mallarmé celebrated in his sonnet "Le tombeau d'Edgar Poe":

> Tel qu'en Lui-même enfin l'éternité le change,
> Le Poète suscite avec un glaive nu
> Son siècle épouvanté de n'avoir pas connu
> Que la mort triomphait dans cette voix étrange!

Eux, comme un vil sursaut d'hydre oyant jadis l'ange
Donner un sens plus pur aux mots de la tribu
Proclamèrent très haut le sortilège bu
Dans le flot sans honneur de quelque noir mélange.

Du sol et de la nue hostiles, ô grief !
Si notre idée avec ne sculpte un bas-relief
Dont la tombe de Poe éblouissante s'orne

Calme bloc ici-bas chu d'un désastre obscur,
Que ce granit du moins montre à jamais sa borne
Aux noirs vols du Blasphème épars dans le futur.

As Eternity at last translates him to Himself, so
The Poet stirs with an unsoiled sword
His epoch terrified for not having known
How death was triumphing in that strange voice.

Like a spastic mob having heard an angel
Transport their vulgar language into glory, they
Loudly proclaim it all a witch's brew drunk
From the dregs of a trashy odious concoction.

And if from that hostile earth and sky our wretched
Hopes cannot erect an eidolon fit
To ornament the glorious tomb of Poe,

That cryptic form of some dark hell-bent disaster,
May this stone shape anyhow raise a wall against
All coming septic pieties and profane expectorations.[3]

Poe's "désastre obscur" is the representation of perpetuated loss that Mallarmé celebrates in "Le tombeau d' Edgar Poe." His pursuit and display of supreme artifice is the negative image of the poetic commitment to "Supernal Beauty." For it is not art that triumphs in the strange of voice of Poe, it is a triumphant death ("que la mort triomphait dans cette voix etrange"). An exquisite play on the word "que" signals not just the factive assertion *that* death triumphs—that poetry fails, that poets are cursed—but equally important, *how* death triumphs. Death triumphs not as mortality but as the artifice of mortality, the poetic revelation of Death's truth, not least of all its poetic truth: the failure of poetic aspiration, which then becomes, as always in Poe, the artifice that protects Eternity from profanation.

Like William Carlos Williams, Mallarmé has perceived how Poe draws a purer sense from the vulgate of his American language. Poe forces readers to experience American English as strange, as *es*tranged. The interpretive question in Poe therefore becomes not *what* it means but *how* it means, and so far as readers are concerned in that action, how they make equivalent meanings. Mallarmé makes an equivalent meaning by writing his sonnet, where he demonstrates how ordinary language gets purified. "Que" in line 4 illustrates how language must be worked so that it differs from itself, but "avec" in line 10 is an even more spectacular illustration. The word is acutely denatured, functioning here simultaneously as a preposition (for "Du sol et de la nue hostiles"), an adverb (with "sculpte"), and the apparition of an adjective (in its position in the line).

Strange to say, this strange new kind of poetry lifts up even those who have no understanding of its catastrophic import ("suscite . . . son siècle epouvanté" etc). For if Poe—like any artist—cultivates a meticulous craftsmanship, he is yet simply a mortal person who cannot fail to fail of his poetic aspirations: as Dante wrote, he has the habit of art and a hand that shakes ("ch'a l'abito de l'arte ha man che trema"). To write in this way, with this conscious understanding, is to glorify the vulgar dialects of poetic aspiration, their inordinate desires and their daily breath. Precisely, as Mallarmé avers, "donner un sens plus pur aux mots de la tribu"—showing *how* Poe did *that* by doing it again in the dialect of a different tribe.

That is what Williams meant when he said Poe was "the beginning" of American poetry. Poe—or rather, Poe's writing—was itself "the New World" (Williams 221) and not simply because Poe was what Swinburne told Mallarmé, "the first" American poet.[4] His priority springs from a deeper conviction: that the world—every world—is reborn in a poetic reimagination of the world. "Beginning again and again," as Gertrude Stein wrote in *Composition as Explanation*.

Notes

Index

Notes

Introduction

1. He did this in a conversation with William Dean Howells: see Edwin Watts Chubb, *Stories of Authors British and American* (London: Sturgis and Walton Company, 1910), 285.

2. See Edmund Wilson, "Poe at Home and Abroad," *New Republic* 49, no. 627 (December 8, 1926): 77–80, and "Poe as a Literary Critic," *Nation* 155, no. 18 (October 31, 1942): 452–453.

3. "From Poe to Valéry," *Hudson Review* 2, no. 3 (Autumn, 1949): 327–342. For a useful comprehensive assessment of Eliot's lifelong interest in Poe see B. R. McElderry, "T. S. Eliot on Poe," *Poe Newsletter* 2, no. 2 (April 1969): 32–33.

4. *The Renaissance: Studies in Art and Poetry* (London: Macmillan and Co., 1910), 135.

5. Whitman's essay, "Edgar Poe's Significance," was published in *Specimen Days and Collect* (see *Walt Whitman: Poetry and Prose,* ed. Justin Kaplan (New York: The Library of America, 1996), 896–898). Williams' "Edgar Allan Poe" is the climactic section of *In the American Grain* (1925). Below I cite Whitman from the Library of America edition; Williams is cited from the recent New Directions edition with an Introduction by Rick Moody and with an Afterword by Horace Gregory (New York, 2009), 216–233.

6. *The Swinburne Letters*, ed. Cecil Y. Lang (New Haven: Yale UP, 1959–1962): 2. 370.

7. Poe's interest in Crichton was sparked by William Harrison Ainsworth's historical novel *Crichton,* published in 1836.

8. David Ketterer, *The Rationale of Deception in Poe* (Baton Rouge: Louisiana State University Press, 1979).

9. "Letter to B———," *CT* 7.

10. An interesting fact: Coleridge sets both the "Kubla Khan" Preface and the relevant historical fictions of chapter X of the *Biographia* in a context of drug taking.

11. "Central Self" references Patricia Ball's seminal study of Romantic poetic address: *The Central Self. A Study in Romantic and Victorian Imagination* (London: Athlone Press, 1968). *Un autre* references Rimbaud's famous letter to Georges Izambard (13 May 1871) in which he sketches a program for an unmediated form of poetry (*Oeuvres Complètes*, ed. Antoine Adam (Paris: Gallimard, 1972), 246–249). Though he studied and admired Poe, he never suggested that the American was the first to establish a model for what he wanted.

12. Whitman, "Edgar Poe's Significance," 896.

13. Jonathan Elmer, *Reading at the Social Limit: Affect, Mass Culture, and Edgar Allan Poe* (Stanford: Stanford University Press, 1995).

14. "From Poe to Valéry," *Hudson Review* 2, no. 3 (Autumn 1949): 327, 342.

15. Some basic resources for studying Poe, popular culture, and the graphic arts are Burton Pollin, *Images of Poe's Works: A Comprehensive Descriptive Catalogue of Illustrations* (Greenwood Press: Westport, CT, 1989); Don G. Smith, *The Poe Cinema: A Critical Filmography of Theatrical Releases Based on the Works of Edgar Allan Poe* (McFarland: Jefferson, NC, 1999); Derek Parker Royal, "Sequential Poe-try: Recent Graphic Narrative Adaptations of Edgar Allan Poe," *Poe Studies/Dark Romanticism* 39–40 (2007–2008); M. Thomas Inge, *The Incredible Mr. Poe: Comic Book Adaptations of the Works of Edgar Allan Poe 1943–2007* (Edgar Allan Poe Museum: Richmond, VA, 2008).

16. Yvor Winters, *Primitivism and Decadence: A Study of American Experimental Poetry* (New York: Arrow Editions, 1937).

1. Poe *In Propria Persona*

1. *The Swinburne Letters,* ed. Cecil Y. Lang (New Haven: Yale UP, 1959–1962), 3. 12. (letter of 20 February 1875).

2. The key essay is the famous "From Poe to Valéry," *Hudson Review* 2, no. 3 (Autumn 1949): 327–342. See also B. R. McElderry Jr., "Eliot and Poe," *Poe Newsletter* 2, no. 2 (April 1969): 32–33, where McElderry tracks Eliot's lifelong fascination with Poe.

3. Least of all do we want to lose sight of Poe's firmly reactionary social views. His critical insight into the cultural and political character of the United States gains its purchase through their agency, as I shall discuss below in Chapter 4. Still fundamental is Ernest Marchand's "Poe as Social Critic," *American Literature* 6 (1933–1934): 28–43.

4. See Scott Peeples, *The Afterlife of Edgar Allan Poe* (Rochester, NY: Camden House, 2004).

5. *A Fable for Critics* (G. P. Putnam: New York, 1848), 59.

6. "Edgar Poe's Significance," in *Specimen Days,* ed. Floyd Stovall (New York: New York UP, 1963), 230–233. See also the discussion below in chapter 4.

7. For texts and introductions to the *Marginalia*, see Burton R. Pollin, ed., *The Collected Writings of Edgar Allan Poe,* vol. 2, *The Brevities* (New York: Gordian Press, 1985); and Miller's edition, here cited as *M.* See also Stephen Rachmann's interesting discussion of Poe's *Marginalia* in his "Es lässt sich nicht schreiben: Plagiarism and 'The Man of the Crowd,'" in Shawn Rosenheim and Stephen Rachmann, eds., *The American Face of Edgar Allan Poe* (Baltimore: Johns Hopkins UP, 1995), 60–70. The standard scholarly treatment of the topic is Heather J. Jackson's *Marginalia: Readers Writing in Books* (New Haven, CT: Yale UP, 2001), though Poe, who has an explicit and important theory of marginalia, does not figure prominently in her study.

8. See Joan Dayan on Poe's "Analytic of the Dash," *Fables of Mind. An Inquiry into Poe's Fiction* (New York: Oxford UP, 1987), chapters 1–3.

9. In his celebrated essay "Hamlet and his Problems" (1921), Eliot judged Shakespeare's play a failure because it did not supply objective dramatic equivalents for Hamlet's state of mind—in Poe's terms, "counterfeit" figures. Poe judges that Shakespeare did.

10. "Sweet sounds" is a technical term that Poe uses in "The Rationale of Verse." Swinburne's "Anactoria" contains a virtual commentary on the prosodic meaning of the word "sweet" (a meaning that has been virtually lost to scholarly awareness, if one is to judge by the recent and often excellent studies of prosody and versification). See Thomas Doubleday, "On the Sweetness of Versification," *Blackwood's Magazine* 7 (September 1820): 641–644.

11. Harold Bloom has assigned the term "capable imagination" to the characteristic moves of Romantic figuration. See his study *Figures of Capable Imagination* (New York: Seabury Press, 1976). "Something far more deeply interfused" references to reverse Wordsworth's famous invocation of the Romantic Sublime in "Tintern Abbey," 96.

12. I reference Shelley's famous lament in "A Defence of Poetry" that "When composition begins, inspiration is already on the decline, and the most glorious poetry that has ever been communicated to the world is probably a feeble shadow of the original conceptions of the poet." Poe's "The Philosophy of Composition" is a forceful refusal of such a view.

13. For a good discussion of Rimbaud's trope of the child, see Edward J, Ahearn's *Rimbaud, Visions and Habitations* (Berkeley: University of California Press, 1983), chapter 1.

14. Poe means *all* of the treatises, but most of all Charles Babbage's unauthorized "Ninth," written (1837) to comment critically on the original eight treatises commissioned (1833) by the Earl of Bridgewater. The essays were each written to demonstrate the truth of Natural Religion, i.e., that God was subject to human understanding. Poe regarded such ideas as preposterous.

15. Poe is using the translation of Thomas Tracy. I quote from a later (anonymous) translation adapted from Tracy and published with an introduction by Charlotte Yonge (available online: http://www.fullbooks.com /Undinex94121.html).

16. This is Poe's phrase in *Eureka* for the material creation.

17. That is, "The Conversation of Eiros and Charmion," "The Colloquy of Monos and Una," and most important, "The Power of Words," which was the last he wrote.

18. Poe made a clear forecast of this marginalium two years earlier in the tale "Mesmeric Revelation" (which he sometimes called "Last Conversations of a Somnambule"). Though a "fable," as he told an unnamed correspondent in April 1846, "Mesmeric Revelation" was a work in which "actual truth [was] involved." He must have been referring to the experiments he reports in the marginalium. I cite here from the edition of Poe's letters in Jeffrey Savoye's *The Edgar Allan Poe Society of Baltimore. Works. Letters* because this is the most correct and up-to-date edition available, superseding the available print editions: http://www.eapoe.org/works/letters/index.htm.

19. In his "A Defence of Poetry: see *Shelley's Poetry and Prose,* ed. Donald H. Reiman and Sharon B. Powers (New York: W. W. Norton, 1977), 482.

20. I reference Poe's important angelic dialogue of this title, which although a fiction, is also a philosophical investigation.

21. For an interesting recent discussion of this topic, see Elizabeth Duquette, "Rethinking American Exceptionalism," *Literature Compass* 10 (2013): 473–482.

22. "Auguries of Innocence," *The Complete Poetry and Prose of William Blake,* rev. ed. David V. Erdman, commentary by Harold Bloom (New York: Anchor Books, 1988), 493.

23. The quotation is from Blake's *Four Zoas,* "Night the Ninth" (ibid. 403).

24. Paradoxical though it might seem, Poe's method mirrors what Barton Levi St. Armand some years ago analyzed as Poe's "Metaphysic of Gnosticism." See "Poe and the Metaphysic of Gnosticism," *Poe Studies* 5, no. 1 (June 1972): 1–8. To his acute study I would only add that Poe's gnostic forms necessarily operate in a discourse of Fear, and that the ultimate liberation they promise is for Poe unattainable. The environment of Fear in which Poe's works operate is at once the reflex of a soul bound to a wheel of fire and an emblem of the soul's grandeur for having made the conscious choice.

25. See Keats's letter to John Taylor, 27 February 1818.

26. See *The Soul of Rumi: A New Collection of Ecstatic Poems,* trans. with an Introduction and Notes by Coleman Barks (New York: Harper, 2001): 176, 191–192.

27. See the discussion below of the conclusion of *Eureka.* Poe's figure has a good deal in common with Blake's apocalyptic vision as it is presented in *The*

Marriage of Heaven and Hell, The Four Zoas, and the prose commentary
A Vision of the Last Judgment. But of course Poe would have had access to
none of those works.

2. Poetics and Echopoetics

1. For Winters, see the discussion below. Laura Riding, "The Facts in the
Case of Monsieur Poe," *Contemporaries and Snobs* (London, 1928); T. S.
Eliot, "From Poe to Valéry," *The Hudson Review* 2, no. 3 (Autumn 1949):
327–342.

2. Published in *American Literature* 8, no. 4 (January 1937): 379–402.

3. "For, in regard to Passion, alas! its tendency is to degrade, rather than to
elevate the Soul. Love, on the contrary—Love—the true, the divine Eros—the
Uranian, as distinguished from the Dionæan Venus—is unquestionably the
purest and truest of all poetical themes. And in regard to Truth—if, to be sure,
through the attainment of a truth, we are led to perceive a harmony where none
was apparent before, we experience, at once, the true poetical effect—but this
effect is referable to the harmony alone, and not in the least degree to the truth
which merely served to render the harmony manifest." "The Poetic Principle"
(paragraph 34).

4. Here I will be pointing out only some of the more dramatic mock-
serious moments in the essay. Many more could and should be exposed and
examined. The essay's fundamental working distinction between verse and
poetry is especially important since it introduces a running commentary on
all of the essay's examples of verse technique.

5. Reconsidering Poe's "Rationale of Verse," *Poe Studies: History, Theory,
Interpretation,* 44 (2011): 69–86.

6. See Richard Fletcher, *The Stylistic Development of Edgar Allan Poe.*
(The Hague: Mouton, 1973), 10; Charles Feidelson, *Symbolism and American
Literature* (Chicago: U. of Chicago Press, 1953), 38–39).

7. See his letter to Stedman cited above, Chapter 1, n. 1.

8. See Poe's review of Thomas Moore's *Alciphron* in *Edgar Allan Poe:
Essays and Reviews* (New York: Library of America, 1984), 333–341.

9. Richard Wilbur, "The House of Poe," Library of Congress Anniversary Lecture of 1959, reprinted in *Edgar Allan Poe. Critical Assessments,* ed. Graham Clarke (East Sussex: Helm Information, 1991), 235.

10. The word is usually glossed as a derived form from the noun "porphyrogenite" (which Poe probably knew through Byron). But Poe's derived form is an inventive transformation made via the recent language of Natural Philosophy.

11. The suffix is used to form nouns that participate in a productive process, as with the word hydrogen. A notable feature of such nouns is that they can be either the source of the action (oxygen) or the result (parthenogen)—either causative or consequential.

12. The standard discussion of this matter is John Irwin's *The Symbol of the Egyptian Hieroglyphics in the American Renaissance* (New Haven, CT: Yale UP, 1980). While readers of the prose have followed up on Irwin's work, its aesthetic ground in the poetry and poetics remains largely ignored. Michael Williams, for example, shows how Poe uses phonetic wordplay in "The Gold-Bug" ("'The *language* of the cipher': Interpretation in 'The Gold-Bug,'" *American Literature* 53, no. 4 (1982): 108–222, especially 217. Poe himself specifically refers to Champollion's phonetic hieroglyphs in "Some Words for a Mummy."

13. Stuart Levine. *Edgar Poe: Seer and Craftsman.* (DeLand, FL: Everett/ Edwards Inc., 1972), 17–47, especially 38–42.

14. Two options—by no means the only ones—are offered by Keats (PORphyrO) and Browning (PorPHYRo).

15. While Bernstein has been practicing an Echopoetics for a long time—from the beginning, in fact—he has only recently been talking specifically about an echo poetics. His new book of poetry, *Recalculating* (Chicago: University of Chicago Press, 2013), sports a dazzling array of echoic and translational poems. He discusses his views in an especially lucid way in a 2010 interview with Alan Gilbert: http://www.fsgpoetry.com/fsg/2010/04/alan -gilbert-interviews-charles-bernstein.html.

16. Mallarmé's commentary on the mock-seriousness of "The Philosophy of Composition" remains standard: see his *Oeuvres completes,* ed. Henri Mondor et G. Jean-Aubry (Paris: Gallimard, 1945): 229–230.

17. See Wordsworth's "Preface" to the *Lyrical Ballads;* Byron's remark comes in a letter to his friend John Cam Hobhouse of 8 June 1820 (*Byron's Letters and Journals,* ed. Leslie A. Marchand (Cambridge: Harvard University Press, 1973–), 115.

18. In alphabetical order, I would cite the following: Joan Dayan, *Fables of Mind. An Inquiry into Poe's Fiction* (New York: Oxford UP, 1987, chapters 1–3; Alex Gelfert, "Observation, Inference, and Imagination: Elements of Edgar Allan Poe's Philosophy of Science," forthcoming in *Science and Education,* http://www.academia.edu/2060471/Observation_Inference_and_Imagination_Elements_of_Edgar_Allan_Poes_Philosophy_of_Science; W. C. [William Conley] Harris, *E Pluribus Unum* (Iowa City: University of Iowa Press, 2005), chapter 1 (on *Eureka*), pp. 37–70; Susan Manning. "'The Plots of God Are Perfect': Poe's 'Eureka' and American Creative Nihilism," *Journal of American Studies* 23, no. 2 (August 1989): 235–251; Susan Welsh. "The Value of Analogical Evidence: Poe's *"Eureka"* in the Context of a Scientific Debate," *Modern Language Studies* 21, no. 4 (Autumn, 1991): 3–15. For Paul Valéry, see his "On Poe's *Eureka*," in *The Collected Works of Paul Valéry,* vol. 8, ed. Jackson Mathews, trans. Malcolm Cowley and James Lawler (Princeton: Princeton University Press, 1968): 161–176.

19. *The Marriage of Heaven and Hell,* plate 22.

20. Most important is the following passage from "The Poetic Principle," whose pertinence will be discussed in my commentary on *Eureka* (where the topic of poetic consistence will be addressed): "With as deep a reverence for the True as ever inspired the bosom of man, I would nevertheless, limit, in some measure, its modes of inculcation. I would limit to enforce them. I would not enfeeble them by dissipation. The demands of Truth are severe. She has no sympathy with the myrtles. All *that* which is so indispensable in Song, is precisely all *that* with which *she* has nothing whatever to do. It is but making her a flaunting paradox, to wreathe her in gems and flowers. In enforcing a truth, we need severity rather than efflorescence of language. We must be simple, precise, terse. We must be cool, calm, unimpassioned. In a word, we must be in that mood which, as nearly as possible, is the exact converse of the poetical. *He* must be blind, indeed, who does not perceive the radical and chasmal differences between the truthful and the poetical modes of inculca-

tion. He must be theory-mad beyond redemption who, in spite of these differences, shall still persist in attempting to reconcile the obstinate oils and waters of Poetry and Truth" (*CT* paragraph 11).

21. See also Scott Peeples's view that *Eureka* is less "a theory of the known universe [than] a parallel universe created by Poe" (188), and George Kelly's comment that the poem is "a cosmology based upon aesthetic theory" (quoted in David Wagenknecht, *Edgar Allan Poe. The Man Behind the Legend* (New York: Oxford University Press, 1963): 219).

22. The letter is a truncated form of the satiric hoax Poe wrote in 1848, "Mellonta Tauta."

23. *Eureka*'s most concentrated illustration of these processes comes in paragraphs 180–188.

24. See in particular Jonathan Taylor, "Cosmology and Cosmogony," in *Edgar Allan Poe in Context,* ed. Kevin J. Hayes (Cambridge: Cambridge University Press, 2013), 353–362; see also Arthur Hobson Quinn, *Edgar Allan Poe: A Critical Biography* (New York: D. Appleton-Century Co., 1941), 553–557.

25. See Ilkka Niiniluoto, "Abduction and Geometrical Analysis: Notes on Charles S. Peirce and Edgar Allan Poe," in *Model-Based Reasoning in Scientific Discovery,* ed. Lorenzo Magnani, Nancy J. Nersessian, and Paul Thagard (Kluwer Academic: New York, 1999), 239–254; and Alex Gelfert, "Observation, Inference, and Imagination: Elements of Edgar Allan Poe's Philosophy of Science [forthcoming in *Science and Education,* http://www.academia.edu /2060471/Observation_Inference_and_Imagination_Elements_of_Edgar _Allan_Poes_Philosophy_of_Science.

26. Unlike Keats, Poe insists on the importance of irritability in the human effort to engage Supernal Beauty: see the central paragraph (11) in "The Poetic Principle." For Keats, however, negative capability—a form of wise passiveness— is a condition of entire affective satisfaction: see his famous letter to his brothers of 21 December 1817.

27. If Jennifer Greeson is right in her reading of that phrase as a coded reference to the United States (U[niverse of] S[tars]), *Eureka* becomes what she takes it to be: Poe's dark commentary on the historical condition of "America." See her essay "Poe's 1848: Eureka, the Southern Margin, and the Expanding U[niverse] of S[tars]," in *Poe and the Remapping of Antebellum Print Culture,*

ed. J. Gerald Kennedy and Jerome McGann (Baton Rouge: Louisiana State University Press, 2012): 123–142.

28. Dante Gabriel Rossetti, "The Portrait," 11. The sonnet is an ominous celebration of the Beatricean muse that presides over Rossetti's mournful and never-ending remembrance of loss.

3. Poetry: or Masks for a Read Death

1. And continue to be. The discussion has scarcely ended with Mabbott's 1978 excellent notes, which summarize the commentaries that descended into his hands. See Mabbott 166–169.

2. Both Baudelaire and Swinburne picked up on Poe's configuration. See "L'Héautontimorouménos" 21–22 ("Je suis la plaie et le couteau!/ Je suis le soufflet et la joue!), and "Hertha" 21–25 ("I the mark that is miss'd/ And the arrows that miss,/ I the mouth that is kiss'd/ And the breath in the kiss,/ The search, and the sought, and the seeker, the soul and the body that is."

3. See Blake's Proverb of Hell, "Everything possible to be believed is an image of Truth." Keats: letter to Benjamin Bailey, 22 November 1817. Stein, *Composition as Explanation* (London: Hogarth Press, 1926).

4. Coleridge's discussion is in fact an effort to marry a psychological theory to an ontological theory (e.g., "'What is *poetry?*' is so nearly the same question with, what is a poet?" etc. (*Biographia Literaria*, chapter 14). See above, Chapter 2.

5. In terms of the English tradition, where the form of the dramatic monologue was established, the difference is marked by the monologue form as shaped by Tennyson or by Browning. While scholars take Browning as normative, there is no question but that Tennyson's model was far more productive for poets, as the cases of Rossetti, Swinburne, Webster, Pound, and Eliot prove.

6. The only exceptions are revealing: "The Haunted Palace" and "The Conqueror Worm," the former the composition on Roderick Usher (in "The Fall of the House of Usher"), the latter of Ligeia (in "Ligeia"). In each case, Poe supplies a particular referential context for the poems, encouraging us to read them in expressive terms. As separately published they are, psychologically, what

Baudelaire calls "*lyrique anonym.*" For a discussion of this kind of "anonymous" lyric mode, see McGann, "Byron and the Anonymous Lyric," *Byron and Romanticism* (Cambridge: Cambridge University Press, 2002), 93–112. And for further comment on Poe's decisive move against the conventions of nineteenth-century poetry, see below the discussion of "Sonnet—to Science."

7. It is worth remarking *en passsant* that this structure in "The Raven" is exactly replicated in the tales "The Fall of the House of Usher" and "Ligeia." Because these are Poe's signature prose works, this formal symmetry marks a central pattern that can be traced throughout Poe's writings.

8. Poe's formulation is "the reciprocity of cause and effect." The phrase first appears in the *Marginalia* of 1 November 1844, whence Poe appropriated it for his review of "The American Drama" (1845). The idea is fundamental to the design of *Eureka*. See Miller's edition of the *Marginalia, M* 9–10 and *ER op. cit.,* 365–368; see also Terence Whalen's discussion on Poe's thought here and its relation to "The Power of Words" in *Edgar Allan Poe and the Masses. The Political Economy of Literature in Antebellum America* (Princeton: Princeton UP, 1999), 253ff.

9. Mabbott points out (179) that her name echoes the Greek word for peace (εἰρήνη *(eirēnē)*). But the unusual syllabification echoes the name of the early Greek poetess Erinna and represents as well a variant of the word Erin, the eponymous goddess of Ireland.

10. See Herodotus, *The Histories* Book 7. I make that reference because our contemporary understanding of dreams is so fundamentally conceptual, in contrast to the way dreams appear in ancient texts like Herodotus. Poe's "Destinies" are marked as seriously primitive.

11. See his discussion of fancy and imagination in his review of Moore's *Alciphron* (*ER.* 333–334, 338). Though he calls Moore a poet of the fancy, his gifts in that mode are so supreme, Poe says, that the effect is finally imaginative.

12. Collapsing the Platonic and Aristotelian distinction between two kinds of "making," *techne* and *poiesis,* Poe's work anticipates the program of poetic Objectivism, perhaps especially as it was understood by William Carlos Williams, a passionate admirer of Poe. Rimbaud's celebrated poetic innovations have much in common with Poe's (see Rimbaud's letter to Paul Demeny,

15 May 1871: *Oeuvres Complètes*, ed. Antoine Adam (Paris: Gallimard, 1972), 249–254.).

13. See David Porter's discussion of these kinds of Dickinson poems in *Dickinson. The Modern Idiom* (Cambridge MA: Harvard University Press, 1981), 40–42.

14. "And the angel Israfel, whose heart-strings are a lute, and who has the sweetest voice of all God's creatures."

15. The center of the Gold Rush was the area soon named Eldorado County (early in 1850).

16. "Von Kempelen and his Discovery" was Poe's hoaxing effort to satirize the Gold Rush mania; see his letter to Evert Duyckinck, 8 March 1849.

17. This replicates the moment in "The Descent into the Maelstrom" when the narrator, accepting the fatality of his situation, is finally able to free his mind and begin to see with real clarity.

18. In a private correspondence, J. Gerald Kennedy has added a useful comment on these words: "The names work because they resonate with adjectives that aren't used but are merely intimated: "awe-bear[ing]" and "weird." The actual use of such words would seem affected, but because the reader performs this work intuitively, the ideas emerge from the poetical unconscious."

19. Roman Jakobson remarked on the words' symmetry in "Linguistics and Poetics" (see Chapter 4 n. 14).

20. This is one of the key points in Sarah Helen Whitman's important early essay on Poe, *Edgar Poe and his Critics* (New York: Rudd & Carleton, 1860).

21. See Benjamin's "Theses on the Philosophy of History. IX," in *Illuminations* (New York: Knopf Doubleday, 1968), 257.

22. Christian theological commentaries on the "comedy" of Christian redemption provide an extremely useful template for reading Poe. See for example Jessica N. DeCou, "'Too Dogmatic for Words?' Karl Barth's Comic Theology in Dialogue with the Comedy of Craig Ferguson," *Religion and Culture Web Forum* (February 2011): 1–29; M. Conrad Hyers, *The Spirituality of Comedy: Comic Heroism in a Tragic World* (New Brunswick, NJ: Transaction Publishers, 1996); Ralph C. Wood. *The Comedy of Redemption: Christian Faith and Comic Vision in Four American Novelists* (Notre Dame, IN: University of Notre Dame Press, 1988).

23. The poem as left to us by Poe may reasonably be read with or without the tenth stanza he removed at the request of Mrs. Whitman (though he and Mrs. Whitman both later decided it should be restored). See Mabbott 423n.

24. See "Come Down, O Maid," 30.

4. The Politics of a Poetry without Politics

1. "Taking Poe Seriously," *Georgia Review* 58, no. 4 (2004): 809.

2. See Herbert Tucker, *Tennyson and the Doom of Romanticism* (Cambridge: Harvard University Press, 1988).

3. See Richard Godden's psychoanalytic reading of "The Raven," "Poe and the Poetics of Opacity: or, Another Way of Looking at that Blackbird," *ELH* 67, no. 4 (2000): 993–1009. Godden tracks the poem's intricate phonosemantic webwork in order to argue that the trauma of American slavery is the secret didactic core of the poem's meaning. While Godden's phonosemantic discussion is remarkably incisive, his final move to "solve" the poem's obscurity represents a didactic retreat from the intransigent stance that the poem takes toward any pretension to enlightenment.

4. Reviewing *The Bridge* in 1927 in *Poetry,* Winters remarked that the pursuit of such writing would be "a public catastrophe." The commentary was reprinted by Winters in his study *Primitivism and Decadence: A Study of American Experimental Poetry* (New York: Haskell House, 1937): 13–14.

5. See David Porter, *Emily Dickinson. The Modern Idiom* (Cambridge: Harvard University Press, 1981). 40–42.

6. See Hart Crane, *White Buildings,* Foreword by Allen Tate (New York: Boni and Liveright, 1926).

7. The standard treatment of the ideology of "True Womanhood" is Barbara Welter's *Dimity Convictions: The American Woman in the Nineteenth Century* (Athens: Ohio University Press, 1977).

8. See Larry Ceplair, ed., *The Public Years of Sarah and Angelina Grimké: Selected Writings 1835–1839* (New York: Columbia University Press, 1989); Gerda Lerner, *The Grimke Sisters from South Carolina: Pioneers for Women's Rights and Abolition* (New York, Schocken Books, 1971); Mark E. Perry, *Lift*

Up Thy Voice: The Grimke Family's Journey from Slaveholders to Civil Rights Leaders (New York: Viking Penguin, 2002).

9. Ralph Waldo Emerson, "Man the Reformer" (1841), in *The Political Emerson: Essential Writings on Politics and Social Reform,* ed. David M. Robinson (Boston: Beacon Press, 2004).

10. It may be worth recalling here that all textual materials depend for their effects on their multiple historicalities. The general availability of poetry—its "universality"—is a function of those minute particulars.

11. See Whitman's "Edgar Poe's Significance" in *Specimen Days,* ed. Floyd Stovall (New York: New York University Press, 1963), 230–233.

12. See Robert A. Lively, "The American System, a Review Article," *Business History Review* 29 (March 1955): 81–96; Michael Lind, *Hamilton's Republic: Readings in the American Democratic Nationalist Tradition* (New York: Free Press, 1997).

13. Jonathan Elmer's "The Jingle Man: Trauma and the Aesthetic," 31, http://www.indiana.edu/~engweb/faculty/img/books/elmer_jingle.pdf. Elmer is here following closely Roman Jakobson's approach to the phonic elements of poetic expression (for instance in his celebrated essay "Linguistics and Poetics," http://akira.ruc.dk/~new/Ret_og_Rigtigt/Jakobson_Eks_15_F12.pdf. See also Matthew J. Bolton, "Rhyme and Reason in Poe and His Predecessors," in *Critical Insights: The Poetry of Edgar Allan Poe,* ed. S. Frye (Salem MA: Salem, 2010), 60.

14. See *The Works of Thomas Love Peacock,* ed. H. F. B. Brett-Smith and C. E. Jones (New York: AMS Press, 1967) VIII. 20.

15. For an excellent treatment of Shelley's "apocapolitics," see Morton Paley, "Apocapolitics: Allusion and Structure in Shelley's 'Mask of Anarchy,'" *Huntington Library Quarterly* 54, no. 2 (Spring 1991): 91–109.

16. See Shelley's "A Defence of Poetry," in *Shelley's Poetry and Prose,* ed. Donald H. Reiman and Sharon B. Powers (New York: W. W. Norton, 1977), 505.

17. *The Works of Jeremy Bentham,* ed. John Bowring (Edinburgh: William Tait, 1843): 3.346a, 347b.

18. For Shelley's influence on Poe, Julia Power remains fundamental: *Shelley in America in the Nineteenth-Century: His Relation to American*

Critical Thought and His Influence (Lincoln: University of Nebraska Press, 1940), chapter 6.

19. Levine annotates Shelley as the source for the phrase "the desire of the moth for the star" (*CT* 203 n. 14) but leaves unremarked the equally relevant allusion to *Adonais* stanza 43, as well as the pervasive presence of ideas from "A Defence of Poetry."

20. For "the before unapprehended relations of things," see Shelley, "Defence of Poetry," *Shelley's Poetry and Prose*, 482.

21. See "The Poetic Principle" in *CT* 182, paragraph 11.

22. The best readings are by Barbarese, "Taking Poe Seriously," *Georgia Review* 58, no. 4, 109–111; Edward H. Davidson in *Poe: A Critical Study* (Cambridge, MA: Harvard University Press, 1957), 38–39, 108; and David Halliburton, *Edgar Alan Poe: A Phenomenological View* (Princeton: Princeton University Press, 1973): 88–92.

23. I quote Barbarese here because he gives special notice to one of Poe's fundamental moves: to turn narrative form against itself. But while he has (so to speak) had the experience of Poe, he has somewhat missed its meaning—though not by much, as is clear when he discusses Poe in terms of the distinction between Arcadia and Eden. In fact, Poe's Otherworld is neither Arcadia nor Eden; it is "Aidenn"—a postlapsarian region where the measure of spiritual innocence is not adult reflection or rationality but something very like Rimbaud's primitive abduction of unimagined realities.

24. See Mabbott, 179–189. Unnoticed is the reference to Geraldine in Coleridge's "Christabel," for whom the word "bright" is a virtual epithet (it is used eleven times). See also note 26 below for a pertinent Keats allusion. Davidson makes the interesting observation that "The Sleeper" is "modeled rather closely on the burial ritual in the Book of Common Prayer (108). Reading the poem as a revisionary treatment of that work—as central an ideological document as we have in English—would be a fruitful exercise.

25. For a good treatment of the political use of folklore, including the Sleeping Beauty legend, see Christa Kamenetski, *Children's Literature in Hitler's Germany: The Culture Policy of National Socialism* (Athens: Ohio University Press, 1984).

26. The allusion at line 19 to Keats's "Ode to Psyche"—another Sleeping Beauty poem—is even more apparent in the first version of "The Sleeper," "Irenë" (line 23).

27. See Mabbott, 189 note. Davidson (39), I think correctly, suggests that the line is a simple analytic detail. But his view is also a bit disingenuous since more sentimental readers would want to idealize the lady's final state.

28. It is worth mentioning that the passage clearly recalls lines 29–32 of the version of "A Paean" that Poe printed in his 1831 volume *Poems,* where "The Sleeper" was also published in its first version, "Irene." The equivalent passage in "Irene" is lines 67–74, the conclusion of the poem. The text in "A Paean" reads: "Thus on the coffin loud and long/I strike—the murmur sent/Through the grey chambers to my song/ Shall be the accompaniment."

29. I cite Rimbaud because his famous "Lettres du Voyant" (1871) express a critique of the Romantic "I," and a commitment to reasoned vision, that is entirely congruent with Poe's theory and practice.

30. See Mabbott, 181, notes.

31. The Moore reference is to *Lalla Rookh,* "Paradise and the Peri" (n. to line 478); the Shakespeare reference is to *Macbeth* III. 5. 23–29.

32. This is the central point of William Carlos Williams' "Edgar Allan Poe," the key section of *In the American Grain:* "The strong sense of a beginning in Poe is in *no one* else before him" (222).

33. Virgil Nemoianu has mapped the European landscape of this discourse in his splendid study *The Taming of Romanticism: European Literature and the Age of Biedermeier* (Cambridge, MA: Harvard University Press, 1984). His interpretation of the significance of this discourse is quite different from my own.

34. Whitman's "The Sleepers" has a good deal in common with Poe's poem. I sometimes wonder whether he changed its title to "The Sleepers" in 1871 in homage to Poe.

35. *Edgar Poe and his Critics* (New York: Rudd & Carleton, 1860), 48.

36. "The Doom of Romanticism" is the splendid title of Herbert Tucker's splendid study of Tennyson: *Tennyson and the Doom of Romanticism* (Cambridge, MA: Harvard University Press, 1988).

37. William Blake mapped this psychic world of Beulah in his strange epic visions *Milton* and *Jerusalem.*

38. *Literary Democracy: The Declaration of Cultural Independence in America* (New York: Viking Press, 1981), 70, 80, 76.

39. For the Bernardin de Saint-Pierre echo in lines 9–12 see Mabbott, *Poetry*, 90. Poe knew the passage from a translation in an 1808 Philadelphia edition.

40. Christopher Bundrick was the first to note the unusual manipulation of the sonnet form: "Obsessive Poe(tics): Meter and Rhyme in the Poetry of Edgar Allan Poe," a paper from the 85th Commemorative Program (2007) of the Edgar Allan Poe Society of Baltimore. It was published as a pamphlet in 2011 by the Society and is available online: http://www.eapoe.org/papers /psblctrs/pl20071.htm. An essay also relevant to the poem is George Montiero's "Edgar Poe and the New Knowledge," *Southern Literary Journal* 4, no. 2 (Spring 1972): 34–40. Neither perceives the crucial pertinence of the title, which Poe added in 1841 and kept thereafter.

41. One of the more interesting efforts to grapple with the problem of "The Bells" is Jonathan Elmer's "The Jingle Man: Trauma and the Aesthetic."

42. The event is recorded in John H. Ingram, *Edgar Allan Poe: His Life, Letters, and Opinions* (London: John Hogg, 1880): 2.155.

43. Many editions of Poe's poetry do not print the italics, thus refusing Poe's explicit directions. But they are clearly present in the two most authoritative texts of the poem—Mabbott's texts E and F (see Mabbott 435–439). Although text F (the *Richmond Examiner* proofsheets) has often been treated as an unreliable witness, its congruence with text E suggests that its bad eminence is undeserved. The word does not appear at all in the short earlier mss.

44. See Christopher Aruffo, "Reconsidering Poe's 'Rationale of Verse,'" *Poe's Studies* 44 (2011): 69–86.

45. One of the most useful commentaries on the problems of scansion and recitation in Poe is Helen Ensley's "Metrical Ambiguity in the Poetry of Edgar Allan Poe," in *No Fairer Land. Studies in Southern Literature Before 1900*, ed. J. Lasley Dameron and James W. Mathews (Troy, NY: Whitston Publishing Co., 1986): 144–158.

46. Helen Ensley's pamphlet *Poe's Rhymes* (Enoch Pratt Free Library, 1981) has one of the most acute discussions of rhyme and rhythm in Poe. Her analysis and examples show with great clarity how and why one should not

use scansion to map Poe's prosody. Scansion is only useful for providing the technical means of exposing the prosodic opportunities in Poe's poetry.

47. This feature of the poem was pointed out to me by my colleague Herbert Tucker.

48. That was the subtitle of his great unfinished narrative *The Four Zoas.*

49. See J. Gerald Kennedy, *Poe, Death, and the Life of Writing* (New Haven: Yale University Press, 1987), 71; Karen Weeks, "Poe's Feminine Ideal," in *The Cambridge Companion to Edgar Allan Poe*, ed. Kevin J. Hayes (New York: Cambridge University Press, 2002), 152; David Reynolds, *Beneath the American Renaissance: The Subversive Imagination in the Age of Emerson and Melville* (New York: Knopf, 1988), 46; and Adam Bradford, "Inspiring Death: Poe's Poetic Aesthetics, 'Annabel Lee,' and the Communities of Mourning in Nineteenth-Century America," *Edgar Allan Poe Review* 12, no.1 (2011): 73.

50. See Bradford, "Inspiring Death"; and James J. Farrell, *Inventing the American Way of Death* (Philadelphia: Temple University Press, 1980), 42.

51. The first judgment is Bradford's (74), the second Mrs. Frances Osgood's (as quoted in Griswold's "Memoir of the Author" in *The Works of the Late Edgar Allan Poe*, with a "Memoir of the Author" by Rufus Wilmot Griswold (J. S. Redfield, 1850), 3.xxxvii).

52. Harriet Beecher Stowe began the long subsequent process of complicating if not entirely dismantling the Byronic mythology when she published *Lady Byron Vindicated* (Osgood, Fields, & Co.: 1870). Her more brief introduction appeared in the previous year in *The Atlantic Monthly.*

53. Here I give the English-language first lines from D. G. Rossetti 's translations in his epochal 1861 collection *The Early Italian Poets* (1861). But see the discussion below where translations are supplied from English versions that were accessible to Poe.

54. Charles Bernstein, *Recalculating* (Chicago: University of Chicago Press, 2013).

55. See discussion below of Poe's possible sources. The English translations here are taken, alternately, from the two that Poe might have been reading: Charles Lyell's translations in *The Canzoniere of Dante Alighieri* (James Bohn, 1836, 1840); and Theodore Martin's in his extended essay "Dante and Beatrice," *Tait's Edinburgh Magazine* (January 1845): 14–26. Lyell's book is

perhaps the more likely source, but Martin supplies a much more elaborate recapitulation of the *Vita Nuova*.

56. See George Watson, "The First English *Vita Nuova*", *Huntington Library Quarterly* 49 (1986): 401–407.

57. The similarities between the two poems is particularly underscored in their shared references to the "friends" and "kinsmen" of Lenore and Annabel Lee.

58. See Stevens' poem "The Worms at Heaven's Gate," in *Harmonium* (1923), *The Collected Poems of Wallace Stevens* (New York: Knopf, 1967), 49.

59. "Wormy circumstance" is Keats's charmingly ironic phrase for Isabella's gravedigging devotions (see "Isabella: or, The Pot of Basil," stanza 49).

60. Quoted in Griswold's "Memoir," n. xxxvi.

61. I quote from the lamentation of Blake's earth goddess, Enion. See *The Complete Poetry and Prose of William Blake*, ed., David V. Erdman, commentary by Harold Bloom (Berkeley: University of California Press, 1982), 325.

62. Her explicit concern was that people would read the poem as a love tribute to women who were not Poe's wife (see Mabbott's summary of the discussion 473–475).

63. See especially Gary Scott Smith, *Heaven in the American Imagination* (Oxford and New York, 2011), chapters 3, 4.

64. See Bernstein, "The Truth in Pudding," in *Recalculating*, 4.

65. See above, Chapter 1, footnote 10 and the associated discussion of the technical prosodic term "sweet."

66. See *Biographia Literaria*, chapter XVIII, the long footnote in the fourth paragraph where he begins his critique of Wordworth's theory of "metrical composition."

67. Paull F. Baum, *The Other Harmony of Prose: An Essay in English Prose Rhythm* (Duke University Press, 1952). It is impossible to illustrate, in this bibliographical medium, what would be involved in such a prosodic recomposition. See my set of Poe recitations made for PennSound, and in particular the final recitation of "Annabel Lee": http://writing.upenn.edu/pennsound/x /McGann-Poe.php. See also Chris Mustazza, "Re-Rhythm: Jerome McGann's Modern Reading of Poe's 'Annabel Lee'": http://mustazza.blogspot.com/2014 /02/re-rhythm-jerome-mcganns-modern-reading.html.

Coda

1. Swinburne, *Letters,* 2.370.

2. Poe's reference to "the mirrors in the temple of Smirna" is recalling Pliny's description of the "monstrous mirrors" in the Temple at Smyrna (in present-day Turkey), which produced distorted images (see Pliny's *Natural History* 33.45).

3. To Swinburne, who was enthusiastic about the effort to set up a Poe Memorial in Baltimore, the actual structure turned out a travesty—worse even than the effort at the Byron Memorial in London. See Swinburne, *Letters* 3. 260.

4. Ibid.

Index

116–117; speaker or poet in, 116–117, 133–134, 135, 140–145, 159, 160, 161–163, 184–185; content compared to style in, 117–129, 148; performative address or recitation of, 120, 179–180, 182–183, 197, 198–200; of wit or fancy, 123–124; affectation in, 126; significance of unremarkable in, 129; artifice exposed in, 132–133, 149; psychology in, 133–134, 135, 143, 144–145, 162, 174–175, 184–185; human condition in, 136–140; satire in, 137–138; memory in, 139–141, 148, 166–167, 168; time in, 140–143; fear in, 143, 186; Romanticism in, 148; intertextuality of, 149–150, 164, 186–193, 197–198; politics in, 149–150, 154–155, 164, 165–168; misogyny in, 151–152; catastrophe in, 167, 186, 193–194, 197, 204–205; depersonalization of, 172. *See also specific poetry*

Poetry and poetics: Mallarmé on, 1; of Coleridge compared to Poe, 6–7, 91–92; plagiarism in, 7–8, 86–87; human being or action in, 25–26, 185–186; *Hamlet* and revelation of, 26; didacticism in, 27, 34, 36–37, 71, 79, 148, 150, 157, 198; moral in, 27, 42, 156; Poe's writing on aims of, 27–28, 35, 39–40, 64–66, 71–72, 73, 157–158; truth in, 28, 33, 35, 36–37, 71–72, 95, 132, 157; intellect, moral sense, and taste in, 28–29; beautiful and human immortal condition in, 29–30, 39–40; Poe's

writing on definition and nature of, 30–34, 35–37, 86–94, 95–96, 97, 106, 112–113, 167; as response to demand, 31; beauty in defining, 31–32, 33, 34, 36–37, 86–87; rhythm in, 32, 33, 34, 134–135; music or acoustics in, 32–33, 35–36, 55, 64–65, 73, 78, 86–87, 180; performative address or recitation in, 34, 89–90, 183; passion in, 36–37, 38–39, 40, 71–72; supernal desires in, 37–39, 72–73; love in Shelley's, 40–41; cause and effect compared to reciprocity in, 44–45; intellectual content in, 70–72, 90, 114–116, 117–118, 120, 156–157; verse and versification systems in, 75, 77, 78, 86–90, 134–135; impetus to writing, 93–94; Romanticism on relevance of, 97; verse compared to, 106; human condition exposed by, 111–112; Poe's theory on, 116; suffering in, 136, 200; memory and, 148; Nineteenth century, 151–154; politics and, 155–156, 157–158, 165–166; study of, 173–174

Politics and political: in Poe's writing, 9, 146–147, 154, 155–156; in Poe's poetry, 149–150, 154–155, 164, 165–168; in death of beautiful women, 151–152, 158–159; misogyny, 151–152; Poe on American, 155–156; poetry and, 155–156, 157–158, 165–168

Pope, Alexander, 2

ML   11-14